Alienated Nation

The New Quest for Liberty

By

Brooks A. Agnew

Table of Contents

Preface

Why would a scientist and commercial engineer be writing a book about America? Because while I was learning how to create complex manufacturing systems that created jobs for people and made cars and many of the parts that go in them, I discovered a key to sociology. Perhaps even more descriptive would be the realization that the intelligent forces behind national commerce were perhaps not human at all. They were eternal principles that when adhered to could create a nation where all beings could have the liberty to reach their highest potential in mortal form.

Like the indomitable Coriolis Effect[1], this steady force for dominion over the management of value in our society was withstood only by the rotational coordinates of American willpower. "Always in motion, the future is," said the wise Yoda while teaching young Skywalker in the Degoba System. I discovered that the human race's compunction for tyranny wasn't like a quantum foam of infinite possibilities out of which charismatics rise to lead the lost to victory. Rather, there was resonance working inside the chaos of millions of Americans dreaming large and working calendars rather than timeclocks.

It seemed like the sewing of America had been rained upon which the inspiration and fearlessness of gods in embryo. As commanded, men did not return rain to the heavens, but rather planted their souls into the ground and fertilized them with sweat and perseverance to produce nearly unlimited bounty. The spiritual rain soaked the seeds of the divine embryo within each of them, and that best part, that part that does the impossible on a regular basis, thrived and walked through the wilderness with wonder and power.

---

[1] In physics, the **Coriolis effect** is a deflection of moving objects when they are viewed in a rotating reference frame. In a reference frame with clockwise rotation, the deflection is to the left of the motion of the object; in one with counter-clockwise rotation, the deflection is to the right. The mathematical expression for the Coriolis force appeared in an 1835 paper by French scientist Gaspard-Gustave Coriolis, in connection with the theory of water wheels, and also in the tidal equations of Pierre-Simon Laplace in 1778.

I grew up in that rain, when it was pure and almost overwhelming. The ideas flowed into my being like sticking one's finger into an electrical outlet. The vibration and inspiration flashed like pictures and motions and an interconnectedness that cannot be placed into words. I will make a mortal attempt to translate it for this book, so that you can remember who you are and why you are here. There is a reason, after all, that you have picked up this book and are reading these words. Right about now, you are thinking, "Yeah. I know exactly what you are saying."

Lest you think this is in slightest ordinary or mundane, I assure you it is not. It is the most extraordinary discovery in the history of the world, and it has the mathematical divinity to save this country, and perhaps even the world, from lemmingosity. When you fill up your car with gas, you feel that we have somehow stepped onto a side road. When you pay your light bill, or rub your forehead with disbelief in election results you feel it. When you are laid off from your job you feel it. When you walk out of the one-times-ten-to-the-third banks without the funds you need to build your business you feel it. I spoke to the FedEx man today, as he dropped off my most recent order. He looked at my purple 1996 Honda Shadow 1100 and said, "I had to sell my motorcycle last month. I'm 50 years old, and I never used to have trouble paying my bills, but now I had to sell it to make ends meet." When you finish this book, I hope you will know that you are not alone, and that there is something you can do about it.

"Why don't they see this? My idea will work. Why are they so stupid?" you yell inside your car as you loosen your tie after another fruitless meeting with an investor. How many times have you walked out in the noonday Sun and looked up and seen only darkness? How many times have you lurched awake in the early hours with your heart pounding out of your chest, sweating and panting in a lonely realization that you are one paycheck away from being homeless? Unlike the pre-universe void, the solitude in that chamber of responsibility has no peace for you. Fear of failure grips you like a Jehovah Witness dog that has hold of your cuff. You have experienced this, or you would not still be reading.

It gets better. Way better. While I was a college math instructor, I had a chance to do something that most of you never got to do. I experienced the beauty and resonating language of mathematics. Oh, I took the math classes, and I received excellent grades. But I did not really understand the beauty and perfection of the art until I taught it to others. I saw that it was about the relationship between values and the patterns and rates of change that allowed energy to resonate into reality. But the chaotic quantum foam of the universe is not a white noise of innumerable values equally struggling for identity in an eternal sea of unknowns. Far from it.

There are limits to resolution. And with a limited resolution, there needs be a limited universe. I saw that the great physicist, Sir Roger Penrose was mistaken. It was not that consciousness was the result of quantum gravity. No no. It was quite stunningly the beautiful opposite. Quantum gravity was the result of consciousness.

When I was getting my education, I signed up for Calculus. After three weeks, I dropped the class. The instructor was brutal. The student body called him "no mercy Searcy." I almost changed majors, but my love for chemistry drove me through my state of despair until the next semester. I made another attempt, except that this time I walked into a room with a sweet and gentle genius of an Indian professor who taught mathematics like it was music. His understanding of the language was not like that of a drill sergeant, whose awards came by how quickly he could bring a student to tears—yes, there is crying in mathematics—but rather more like Magister Ludi[2]. Each concept was mastered and then inserted into the next concept, and so on. I not only got an "A" in the class, I knew the material. I could hear it. I could feel it. And when I had my ascension experience, I sustained it because I knew the language. With this powerful understanding, I had a new super power. I could walk through the barriers between processes in almost any situation.

Mathematics bequeaths the knowledge—as opposed to *belief*—that there is no such thing as being at rest in the universe. That is to say, you cannot determine how fast a train is moving when you are sitting in one of the

---

[2] *Magister Ludi* by Hermann Hesse. Also titled, *The Glass Bead Game*. Castallia was a school where the relationships between disciplines were distilled to glass beads, collected by students and eventually consolidated into one bead that encompassed all things in the universe.

cars without a window. As a nation, we the people have gone to sleep in the dining car. There are a few *masters* who figured out how to step outside the universe and consider the resolution of the complete set of energy in the universe, almost without being a part of that set. They are trying to wake us up, before the train goes off the cliff. Pretty cool huh?

That is where I am going to take you. I am going to take you outside the universe so you can see what is happening to our nation. If enough of you can be shown what is happening between the lines of our agencies and their regulations, you will be able to reenter the equation of America as a new value and shift the average reality. We need to change the result, because we physicists try to avoid zero and the value of infinite.

The soul of man is not alone. It is connected to everything. When we look out into the night sky, we see mostly the blackness of space and a gathering of stars and planets. With our instruments, we have peered deeper into space than most men have dreamed. The pattern continues as far as photons of light can reach the lens. Without making this book about the study of the velocity of stars or galaxies or clusters, it is important to compare the universe to the saga of the human being and its cyclic sociology.

Earth drifts in a lazy, perfect ellipse around a main sequence star in the outer rim of an average galaxy. For many centuries we held that we were the center of the solar system and the universe. We were told by timeless beings from other worlds throughout our scriptures that we were the solitary creation of God. The very statement belies logic, but then Gnosticism is heresy, is it not?

The soul of man is a social being. We can live alone, doing everything for ourselves, but it's a little like owning a classic car than never comes out of the garage. We are designed to be driven. The progress of the soul is axiomatic to existence, whether we are mortal or not. Nothing is at rest in the universe. For man, the drive is to form social groups and to explore great things. Each mortality provides a soul the chance to master new skills with the biological transducer of the body. Now, whether you believe the human spirit gets one chance to interpret the universe through flesh, or many opportunities on many worlds, makes no difference. The opportunity to deny it will present itself many times, as well as the loss of memory that you ever did so.

Once beings form a social group that facilitates procreation, a community with traditions and histories displays a peculiar and yet repeatable pattern. A tribal energy adds something to the social order of the group. Invariably, positions of specialty service are created and filled with individuals in that tribe. The shaman explains the mysteries of nature and performs healing and prosperity activities for better crops and healthier babies. The biggest and strongest man becomes the tribal commander. The advisors to the commander are remoras—smaller fish that swim with sharks to avoid being picked on by other fish. In each social group there are laborers, midwives, food preparation experts, etc. There are only a handful in each generation who can perceive the universe from outside. They let us know when we have fallen asleep in the train we think is reality.

In this one paragraph is the precursor to nations. Again, a grand and terribly repeatable trait displays itself for the history books to record. For millennia, these social groups very soon hammer their plows into weapons and charge across the misty tundra, hacking to pieces the people of other social groups. Gods of one sort or another have commanded whole communities to annihilate other communities to take their land or their water or their gene pool for their own. The only difference is that now we can make the trip faster, and we can kill thousands with digital insulation from the nightmare of having the blood of a terrified person splattered upon our face. Oh, and we have added oil to the list of national interests for such activities.

I can tell you without doubt whatsoever this one. The soul of man was not made for murder. I know that we have all done it, or are in the process of doing it, or will. Eternity is by design a very long time. Eventually, a soul will grow to the point where it will not harm the mortal life of another soul, but it takes longer than one would think. It is my assertion that mankind on Earth is stepping through a window of evolution for its soul.

Contrary to what have been told on the cable news channels, there is hope for peace on Earth forever from this point forward.

We have reached this precipice before as a race of mortal beings. Man's social zenith has been gleaming in the sun more than once with bright banners snapping in the afternoon breeze. We have consolidated the leadership to only a few, and then one calm and foggy morning those men rowed a small boat across a peaceful bay to inform the other social group that this day would be their last on this Earth. The race of man has walked willingly off the cliff into the smoke and death of war time and time again.

Hopefully, this book will be read in time to turn away from the edge and live.

Foreword

Like you, I was shocked to find out that State and national elections were rigged. Mathematics has such a wonderful way of sampling society and allowing the Republic to digest ideas down to a single representative. That representative is a result of a long string of variables in a local election equation. And, when inserted into the national equation, the *average value,* which we call X-bar or the mean value—no it is not angry, it is simply the average—becomes an even more stable number with we call X-double-bar, or the average of the averages. Amazing and elegant and perhaps even divine in its design, isn't it.

That is unless it continues to give an answer that does not allow lustful men to rise to power. How can you tell the difference between a man who has mastered the art of politics and a man who lusts for power? That, my friends, will be answered in this book.

"Never doubt that a small group of thoughtful, committed citizens can change the world. Indeed, it's the only thing that ever has." Margaret Mead

This book discusses the variables in the equation of the American republic. There are more than a few committed citizens who are trying to change the country, but they are nothing more than road gravel to the agency-government that runs the world. It knows there are more of you than exist in their halls of regulations and enforcement actions, and it fears that you will realize what they are about to accomplish. You know and I know that we have become one nation under surveillance. Everything you buy, surf, or drive past in your car is being watched. Like any prey who knows something is in the grass not far away, you should be very aware that the predator is close.

It knows that when the equation of elections gives an undesired answer there are only two choices. First, those in governmental power can go back and speak to the people again, and sample again, and try to come up with different values to place into the equation. Of course, the beauty of statistics is that the average is very representative of the whole. The larger the set of values, the more stable and more representative the average is going to be. It would take a grand awakening indeed to shift that average value. Changing the average would be difficult and costly, and yet like starlings swimming in the sky we flash as one and move in another direction. That is to say, population-wide shifts in consciousness do occur. It's just that lustful men know only one way to thus twist the collective soul of society. They use the word *fight*.

In our Republic; however, there is a second and much more survivable method of winning elections; cheating. People don't realize that elections are nothing like taking a final math exam with the answers written down on a cheat sheet. One can put the answer on the exam sheet, but unless you show how it was derived—you remember having to show your work in math class—you cannot get full credit. There is a Constitutional process whereby the public has been able to request a review of the voting process to validate that every vote was counted properly. Elections must be traceable. We have to show our work.

The only way to effectively cheat the exam is to remove public review of the votes. In this book, you will discover that is exactly what has taken place.

I was contemplatively Pavlovian about this book for a few election cycles, and then I heard something that brought me to the table, or rather the keyboard. I read that SCYTL, the global leader in secure electronic voting technologies, announced the acquisition of 100% of SOE Software, the leading software provider of election management solutions in the United States.[3]

SCYTL is currently the worldwide leader in the Internet voting space and the acquisition of SOE Software, with its Clarity election management software suite, significantly expands SCYTL's product portfolio beyond

---

[3] SCYTL Acquires SOE Software, Becoming the Leading Election Software Provider
January 11, 2012 7:30 AM EST BALTIMORE & TAMPA, Fla.--(BUSINESS WIRE)--

electronic voting. SCYTL is a technology company specializing in the development of secure electronic voting and election modernization solutions. They are based in Barcelona and with offices in Baltimore, Toronto, New Delhi, Athens, Kiev and Singapore. Furthermore, SOE Software's strong US presence with 900 jurisdictions as customers in 26 states, including 14 state-wide customers, complements very effectively SCYTL's customer base in the United States and internationally with customers in over 20 different countries across 5 continents, including France, Spain, Canada, Norway, Switzerland, South Africa, United Arab Emirates, Mexico, India and Australia.

This means that the votes may be cast in American precincts, but they will be tallied, stored, and reported from a foreign country. The software is so sophisticated, that it has the ability to write code back to the original voting machine to change the vote to match the desired outcome leaving no trace whatsoever. Anonymous voting feeds the fraud perfectly. SCYTL is controlled by several Venture Capital Funds, Nauta Capital, Balderton Capital and Spinnaker. If you know anything about finance, you know that venture capitalists are all about return on investment. Integrity, honesty, and accuracy are not a part of precision, security, and profit.

There is also no possibility, quantum or otherwise, of public review of the voting results. Bingo. Dinner time. Benjamin Franklin once said, "This will be the best security for maintaining our liberties. A nation of well-informed men who have been taught to know and prize the rights which God has given them cannot be enslaved. It is in the religion of ignorance that tyranny begins."

What you will discover about the *Alienated Nation* will enrage you. It may also awaken you to the reality that there is a nefarious will that stood outside the universe and found the alchemical key to usurping the republic formula with their plutarchian solution without your advice or consent. Hopefully, you will do something with that knowledge. The key word is DO. Action. A call to action. Your action. I am already doing mine. You're reading it.

The Founding Fathers

Founders of any successful business have wisdom. Wisdom is not belief or faith. We scientists are often accused of being atheists. We're not. Just because we have to have evidence, does not mean that we are not faithful in the eternality of the human soul. The removal of doubt about the idea that the animated being within our biological transducer is spawned from, if not inextricably connected to, God is a direct observation made by each sentient being.

So we are directly empowered to set up our own living conditions and prosperity. The founding fathers did just that, at great peril to themselves and to more than 100 thousand people who fought in the effort to establish or prevent the birth of America. Building upon their wisdom, we thought we would never be in this position again, but we are.

"A government big enough to supply everything you need is big enough to take everything you have... The course of history shows that as a government grows, liberty decreases." Thomas Jefferson

A direct observation is the definition of a fact. A fact is a scientific term. We scientists collect facts as we go about the process of proving our hypothesis. Evidence is data collected or treated or translated from a measurement device that has been calibrated and certified through ANSI methodologies with standards traceable to those possessed and protected by the National Institute of Standards and Technology.

Knowing all this stuff doesn't make us God. It makes us more like Him, and so we recognize Him when we see Him.

Wisdom is gained through making mistakes. No one ever learned anything by getting everything right. That's why there is crying in mathematics, unlike baseball. The founding fathers were educated and emancipated men who were not necessarily born in the new world. They were forged in the furnaces of King George in England.

The first major action taken to define the role of government, either before or after fighting a war to get to the table in the first place, was the creation of the Magna Carta. Also called Magna Carta Libertatum, is an English charter, originally issued in the year 1215 and reissued later in the 13th century in modified versions. The later versions excluded the most direct challenges to the monarch's authority that had been present in the 1215 charter. The charter first passed into law in 1225; the 1297 version, with the long title (originally in Latin) The Great Charter of the Liberties of England, and of the Liberties of the Forest, still remains on the statute books of England and Wales.

The 1215 charter required King John of England to proclaim certain liberties, and accept that his will was not arbitrary, for example by explicitly accepting that no "freeman" (in the sense of non-serf) could be punished except through the law of the land, a right which is still in existence today. The Magna Carta was the first document forced onto an English King by a group of his subjects, the feudal barons, in an attempt to limit his powers by law and protect their privileges. It was preceded and directly influenced by the Charter of Liberties in 1100, in which King Henry I had specified particular areas wherein his powers would be limited.

One of the 25 barons who created and signed the Magna Carta was Robert de Ros, Lord of Hamlake Castle. He married Isabella Mac William, the illegitimate daughter of William the Lion, King of Scots. When King John came to the throne, he gave Ros the barony of his great-grandmother's father, Walter d'Espec. Soon afterwards he was deputed one of those to escort William the Lion, his father-in-law, into England, to swear fealty to King John. Some years later, Robert de Ros assumed the habit of a monk, whereupon the custody of all his lands and Castle Werke (Wark), in Northumberland, were committed to Philip d'Ulcote, but he soon returned and about a year later he was High Sheriff of Cumberland.

When the struggle of the barons for a constitutional government began, de Ros at first sided with King John, and thus obtained some valuable grants from the crown, and was made governor of Carlisle; but he subsequently went over to the barons and became one of the celebrated twenty-five

14

"Sureties" appointed to enforce the observance of *Magna Carta,* the county of Northumberland being placed under his supervision. He gave his allegiance to King Henry III and, in 1217-18, his manors were restored to him.

Of course, why is this important? Well, not only was Isabella Mac William the illegitimate daughter of the King of Scots, she was the widow of Robert de Bruce. Remember him? Did you ever see the movie *Braveheart*? Okay. Well, Robert de Bruce had a son named Edward. Edward de Bruce had a favorite vassal who controlled and kept safe all of western Scotland whose name was Sir Andrew Agnew. I am a direct descendent of Sir Andrew Agnew of the Agnew Clan from Stranraer, Scotland. The Agnew castle overlooks Loch Naw above Agnew Bay. It was from here that the Hereditary Sheriffs of Galloway protected Rosslyn Chapel and the treasures of the Knights Templar against all enemies. The refiner's fire of tribulation and challenge and failures leading up to the day of success is where wise men are forged.

It was through the Hereditary Sheriffs of Galloway that the Knights Templar kept the Ark of Covenant safe from the greed of men. Many battles were fought to gain the right to sit at that table to make King John sign that Magna Carta. Scots paid the price. Agnews paid that price. That is why we are so few today. Mostly, we were the second to the last man standing. My family's blood is in the ink, as it were, that formed the first Bill of Rights in 1215.

The Magna Carta, as many of you already know, formed the cornerstone of inalienable rights between monarchs and the people. The "Great Charter" drawn up on the field at Runnymede on June 15, 1215 between King John and his feudal barons failed to resolve the crisis that had been brewing in England ever since the death of John's brother King Richard I. Over the long term, however, Magna Carta served to lay the foundation for the evolution of parliamentary government and subsequent declarations of rights in Great Britain and the United States. In attempting to establish checks on the king's powers, this document asserted the right of "due process" of law. By the end of the 13th century, it provided the basis for the idea of a "higher law," one that could not be altered either by executive

15

mandate or legislative acts. This concept, embraced by the leaders of the American Revolution, is embedded in the supremacy clause of the United States Constitution and enforced by the Supreme Court.

To no one will we sell, to no one deny or delay right or justice. After all the language in the Magna Carta, there is no doubt that the Barons did their best to address the grievances of the day. Mostly, these grievances had to do with the overreaching acts of the King and the confiscatory behaviors of the banks. These same grievances endure for 561 more years.

Men and women moved to the wilderness when times got hard. They left their homes and heritage. They left their roots and in many cases their own languages behind. When they reached the ocean, they could go no further. Until men decided to risk sailing off the edge of the world rather than bear the burden of captivity to tyranny another day. Voyages were financed mostly by churches or by monarchs who were promised enormous returns on their investment.

No one knew the way except the Templars. How they got the maps is a matter of legend. The *Flying Scrolls* were stored in Solomon's Temple and flew out of that place in the hands of knights who were sworn to protect them from disclosure. The father-in-law of Christopher Columbus was a direct descendent of the Knights Templar and possessed the map to the West. It was with this map that he convinced Ferdinand and Isabella of Spain to finance his trip to the new world. It took nearly 128 years for people to muster the will to brave death and disease and the loss of everything they owned to make the trip themselves.

The Mayflower Compact was the first governing document of Plymouth Colony. It was written by the colonists, later together known to history as the Pilgrims, who crossed the Atlantic aboard the *Mayflower*. Almost half of the colonists were part of a separatist group seeking the freedom to practice Christianity according to their own determination and not the will of the Anglican Church. It was signed on November 11, 1620 (OS), by 41 of the ship's 101 passengers, while the Mayflower was anchored in what is now Provincetown Harbor within the hook at the northern tip of Cape Cod.

16

The *Mayflower* was originally contracted to land at mouth of the Hudson River, in land granted in a patent from the Crown to the London Virginia Company. The decision was made instead to land farther north, in what is now Massachusetts. This was in some respect a breach of the contract. After all, the Hudson has always been a muddy mess of a river, and the Cape is a spectacularly clean land with calm access to the sea. It was a decision made by a minority leadership and the ship's captain. Why not?

Now, it is important to understand wherein lies the original thorn in the King's side with respect to the colonies. The Compact was with the crown, right? It also had strong religious themes woven into the language. Here it is:

> In the name of God, Amen. We, whose names are underwritten, the loyal subjects of our dread Sovereign Lord King James, by the Grace of God, of Great Britain, France, and Ireland, King, defender of the Faith, etc.
>
> Having undertaken, for the Glory of God, and advancements of the Christian faith and honor of our King and Country, a voyage to plant the first colony in the Northern parts of Virginia, do by these presents, solemnly and mutually, in the presence of God, and one another, covenant and combine ourselves together into a civil body politic; for our better ordering, and preservation and furtherance of the ends aforesaid; and by virtue hereof to enact, constitute, and frame, such just and equal laws, ordinances, acts, constitutions, and offices, from time to time, as shall be thought most meet and convenient for the general good of the colony; unto which we promise all due submission and obedience.
>
> In witness whereof we have hereunto subscribed our names at Cape Cod the 11th of November, in the year of the reign of our Sovereign Lord King James, of England,

France, and Ireland, the eighteenth, and of Scotland the fifty-fourth, 1620.

Was this the same King James that commissioned the assembly of the holy library—Biblio in Latin or Bible in English—that has been the basic scripture from which all Christian churches have been formed for more than 392 years? The very same. The money came from him. The promoters of the voyage made a deal to get themselves to the New World with one goal; to spread the word of God. Do you really believe that?

There are no secrets on a ship. Some of the paying passengers, who were not members of the congregation of religious dissenters leading the expedition, proclaimed that since the settlement would not be made in the agreed-upon Virginia territory, they "would use their own liberty; for none had power to command them...."

To prevent this, many of the other colonists decided to establish a government. The Mayflower Compact was based simultaneously upon a majoritarian model, even though the signers were not in the majority, and the settlers' allegiance to the king. It was in essence a social contract in which the settlers consented to follow the compact's rules and regulations for the sake of survival. That is, until they actually made it to the New World and saw the amazing wealth of resources far from the prying eyes of tax collectors and monarchs.

Did the Compact leaders and ship's captain decide to sail the Mayflower to Massachusetts because the water was cleaner, or because they knew that if they landed outside the terms of the contract with the King, that the contract would be null and void. Instead of preaching, they would be prospecting.

The true American spirit was planted in the soil of Massachusetts by the deepest desire humans can possibly have; the yearning to be free and masters of our own future. 156 years later, the unwritten license to reap the reward of one's own sweat was put into writing. The grievances of 1215 became the grievances of 1776.

Parliament in 1765 passed two acts that produced even greater resentment in the colonies. The Quartering Act required the colonies to house 10,000 British troops in public and even private buildings. The Stamp Act was a form of direct taxation of the colonists. In Boston, New York, Philadelphia, and other cities mass meetings were held in protest. It was argued that Parliament had no right to tax the colonists because they were not represented in that body. Taxation without representation is tyranny!" became the cry.

In modern presidencies, government agencies, departments, and bureaus pass their own regulations, fees, and enforcement action in the form of confiscatory fines, raising hundreds of billions of dollars. The people are not represented in these bodies, which are often layered in secrecy and are exempt from litigation. Many agencies force businesses to submit letters of credit or cash to support the agents sent into those businesses to audit, make assessments, and levy fines. The actions have devastated whole industries that are targeted by the administration.

Too much has already been said about the Stamp Act and the Boston Tea Party, and blah blah blah. You heard it before and it has been played in many games by many players. What I am about to tell you has never been discussed in public. If there is a body of muscle and bone and blood, then this is the artery from pit of darkness.

Kings don't actually do anything. They have generals, who have been groomed and made like any gang member. Being *made,* by the way, is the act of murder to prove one's ability to follow orders of the gang leader. The king issues his orders, and the generals sweep the innocent and solider alike from the face of the Earth like the angels of God. They never question. They never doubt. They never hesitate. They go to their own graves with the absolution on their minds that they were only following orders.

These generals lie, cheat, murder, embezzle, and then parade with their medals and their swords, and their honor, and their military bearing. Kings had earls and dukes and magistrates that carried out his orders and held harmless the king from their actions. No one was responsible for grievous acts, and yet everyone was responsible. The people had no recourse.

The founding fathers had this experience that came from countless battles with lords and counts from all over the kingdom. They knew what would happen if a president was ever afforded this much power without checks and balances. They knew that no one man should be able to command such a force, so they specifically limited the power of the presidency to two men and two men only. The president and vice-president are the Executive Branch. There are no dukes. There are no earls. There are no counts or magistrates who are unelected.

The president is, however, allowed to have a cabinet. [The President] may require the Opinion, in writing, of the principal Officer in each of the executive Departments, upon any subject relating to the Duties of their respective Offices. Without saying so directly, the Constitution created the Cabinet with those words. Note, however, that the Constitution does not go into what the executive departments will be, how many there will be, or what their duties should be.

The first cabinet, that of George Washington, consisted of only four department heads; those of State, Treasury, War, and the Attorney General. The names are familiar: Thomas Jefferson, Alexander Hamilton, Henry Knox, and Edmund Randolph held the offices respectively. What had been four departments became fifteen under President George W. Bush. In the cabinet are also the Vice-President and any other person in the executive department that the President wishes, such as the Ambassador to the U.N. or a National Security Advisor. Since cabinet members are usually department heads, they are appointed by the President and confirmed by the Senate. President Obama has made at least two appointments while the Senate was in session without their advice or consent in direct violation of the Constitution, bringing the total to seventeen cabinet members. Other than confirmation, there are no legal or constitutional requirements for the job. They serve at the whim of the President.

Typically, the cabinet meets on a regular basis, such as weekly. However, because the cabinet is not a legal institution, meetings can be at any interval. In fact, the cabinet may not necessarily ever meet at all. In fact, there need not even be a cabinet. It is only mentioned briefly in the Constitution in Article 2 Section 2.

Article 2 Section 2 says:

> The President shall be Commander in Chief of the Army and Navy of the United States, and of the Militia of the several States, when called into the actual Service of the United States; he may require the Opinion, in writing, of the principal Officer in each of the executive Departments, upon any subject relating to the Duties of their respective Offices, and he shall have Power to Grant Reprieves and Pardons for Offenses against the United States, except in Cases of Impeachment.

> He shall have Power, by and with the Advice and Consent of the Senate, to make Treaties, provided two thirds of the Senators present concur; and he shall nominate, and by and with the Advice and Consent of the Senate, shall appoint Ambassadors, other public Ministers and Consuls, Judges of the supreme Court, and all other Officers of the United States, whose Appointments are not herein otherwise provided for, and which shall be established by Law: but the Congress may by Law vest the Appointment of such inferior Officers, as they think proper, in the President alone, in the Courts of Law, or in the Heads of Departments.

No President knows everything, and he is certainly allowed to have smart people who agree with him to advise him in these areas of specialty. Presidents since Washington have chosen experts to help advise the office. However, these cabinet members, loosely authorized by the Constitution, have morphed over the years into something very much like the arrangement that existed during the reign of the 18th-century King George.

Departmental secretaries are appointed by the President. The people are constitutionally empowered to have advice and consent for these appointments through the Senate in a revised method to keep in check the rise of an unrepresentative form of government. In 2012, President Obama circumvented this process by confirming two agency heads without the advice and consent of the Senate, while the Senate was still in session.

These appointed Secretaries are now more the analog of a Minister, Duke, or Earl following the direct orders of the President. More than 66% of the national budget is spent by these various Ministers of governmental agencies. No taxpaying citizen is represented in any agency in writing regulations, setting fees and creating and executing budgets. This is clearly taxation without representation. One of the founding grievances that inspired colonists to risk everything, including their lives, was the defeat of taxation without representation.

You have heard many state that the Constitution is outdated and that it was not crafted to address a nation with our complexities and of our size and power. This is absolutely false. The founding fathers knew this day would come. It always comes when men rise to power. The founding fathers used their wisdom, gained through generations of tyranny and war, to craft a document that would, if kept intact and defended, keep this type of man from rising to power. They did not need to foresee. They only needed to remember. They built the longest lasting and most inspired republic in history to be inherently resistant to one Branch of government gaining more power than another.

The complexity of America is fabricated. The British Empire was larger than America. It was a widely known fact that the Sun never set on the British Empire. It was powerful and reached to the end of the Earth. The founding fathers were no strangers to global corporations and international banking. They were experts at currency and commerce. They were eloquent thinkers and planners and architects and engineers. They were lovers of the same thing that the original passengers on the Mayflower loved; liberty to make their own future without some dispassionate government leaching off their labors. They knew the leach turns into a vampire.

Benjamin Franklin is quoted as saying, "Democracy is two wolves and a lamb voting on what to have for lunch. Liberty is a well-armed lamb contesting the vote."

Don't think for one moment that they did not envision this day.

The Professional Voter

Benjamin Franklin once said, "When the people find that they can vote themselves money, that will herald the end of the republic."

When someone gets paid to do something, they are a professional. My observation is that you already know we have a few generations of society that court the influence of politicians who will make sure a check shows up every month in the proper amount. The thing I want to make clear is how we got here, and that there is a way out of this era of dependency. It goes both ways, you know. We have an entire political party—we still have a two-party system—that would evaporate into the history books if the process of buying and selling votes was removed.

Roosevelt's New Deal was praised and criticized by politicians, economic experts and businesses during the 1930's and still is today. They were extraordinary times to be sure. Now, we need to talk a little about why the stock market crashed in 1929 in some detail. Suffice it to say that there were two major recessions and then a buildup to a massive stock market fueled by 90% margins—buying stock with a margin account with the low-risk that the market would go up and not down—and the hype of promoters. The middle class was quickly forming and even making the transition to upper class based not on earnings of the public companies, but on the difference between the purchase price and selling price of their stock certificates.

The banks were in on it as well. After all, they had the deposits of their clients with which to gamble. The stage was mostly set by highly leveraged investment positions, extremely high unemployment, and highly inflated stock prices. Keep in mind that all trades were done on the floor of the Exchange. There were no computers programming micro-trades several times a day to stack small returns into large quarterly returns. There was no Federal Deposit Insurance Corporation making sure the deposit were safe up to $100,000 dollars. There was nothing like that. The Crash of 1929 built up slowly and meticulously, as though it was designed from scratch.

America was not in on this alone. In its 14 years following the Great War up to 1933, the Weimar Republic was functional and seemed to be making progress at establishing a Democratic government. As it turns out, it was not the government that was the problem. There were natural forces in society that are well known from millennia of experience.

There were representatives in the Republic who were considered extremists. They battled for supremacy from the pulpit and in the alleyways of the city with knives and guns. The crafters of the Treaty knew full well what they were doing. This Post-war haggling by financiers and politicians fixed German reparations at an annual fee of 132 billion gold marks. This was about one quarter of Germany's total 1921 exports! To no one's surprise, Germany could not make the payments. Germany was forced to use its coal and steel industries to pay the debt. When they defaulted on the payments to the banks, French and Belgian troops moved in and seized the mines and factories. The people responded passively by refusing to work hard. Germany was forced to print money to pay its debts, causing runaway inflation over 1,500%.

The victors of World War I, tried twice to restructure Germany's reparations payments through the Dawes Plan and the Young Plan. The financial burden of reparations was carefully designed and utilized by the international bankers for their own benefit. This was one of the main sources of German discontent that led to acceptance of Hitlerism. The Dawes Plan and later the Young Plan were designed to provide huge amounts of cash that money traders could use in the United States. The micro-trading of cash has long been used by traders to build capital without risk. This capital was utilized in the mid-1920s to create and consolidate the gigantic chemical and steel combinations of I. G. Farben and Vereinigte Stahlwerke, respectively.

Both plans were engineered by these central bankers, who manned the US government committees that managed the reparation plans. The Dawes Plan arranged a series of foreign loans totaling $800 million with their proceeds flowing to Germany. These cartels not only helped Hitler to power in 1933; they also produced the bulk of key German war materials used in World War II.

Even though Germany is technologically the strongest nation in Europe, it did not repay the reparations from the Great War until October 3rd, 2010. The banks made clear and unearned profits from the financing charges. The industrialists and governments received billions every year in cash or valuable commodities for more than 90 years from this Treaty.

One more thing. These industrialists and bankers were forming a military industrial complex—the exact wording of General and President Eisenhower—intent on making money from manufacturing and selling weapons to both sides of the war. Not just one war, but all wars everywhere in the world were the focus of these men. Peace would forever be financially impossible. The greatest and most powerful military machine in history was built is less than 5 years, and was at least 5 years ahead of anything on Earth. When the first test of the Blitzkrieg and Luftwaffe occurred against the Basque town of Guernica on April 26, 1937 by the invitation of Franco, the US military was flying old radial engine technology.

There were no trenches. There were no battle lines. There was only a massive mechanized unit utilizing highly advanced technology, including night-flying, radar-guided aircraft. The raid was over in roughly two days. Tactics included terror bombing and strafing of civilian targets to break the will of the enemy. It was successful in Guernica, and it was successful in Rotterdam in May of 1940 where Holland surrendered in just 6 days. War would never be the same.

While banks and industrialists were making huge profits, the American economy was about to collapse. The stock market had weathered two crippling recessions and come back to record price performance. Trading cash and stocks not on the prospect of earnings, but on the speculated price of the paper itself was driving the perception of value. The perception was there only for the middle class that was pumping everything they had into the market. Chasing the perception of value leveraged the public and the smaller banks to the point that if anything happened to end the ponzi scheme, they would collapse.

The perception did not negatively affect the upper class and industrialists. On the contrary, it cleared the table of all competitors and allowed them to buy up entire industries for pennies on the dollar. The crash was designed. The crash was necessary. The crash only needed to be triggered, like some economic Higgs event, to make the black hole of money explode and create a new universe.

When the crash was triggered, it took place in a matter of days. When the final act occurred, the stock market crashed so hard and so wide that the middle class completely evaporated. By the time the dust settled, there were two classes of Americans. There were billionaires, and there were people working for 25 cents a day and all the potatoes they could carry home.

Within a few days, the middle class went broke. The broke became the poor. The poor became desperate, and then angry, and then hopeless. America was a nation with no hope, because the very foundation of capitalism had been shattered to the ground. People needed a hand up. The wealthy became the theme of Gatsby and Rockefellers and grand industrialists who bought up city blocks and skyscrapers for pennies on the dollar. Oh yeah. I almost forgot to mention. They paid cash. Cash? Who had cash? Exactly my point. The people who had cash had it because they got out of the Market at the peak. They didn't deposit their money in the small banks. They had their own banks. They had real cash coming into their economic powerhouses by financing a war machine that people in the US didn't know about or care about. They had their own steamships to travel to their own banks to get the cash to buy up America. While the people, and the government, scraped garbage cans for lunch, the military industrial corporations walked like the gods across the globe sweeping all opposition out of their way.

President Hoover was an engineer who made a small fortune in mining. He had no former elected office, but he won by a landslide in 1928 against his Democrat opponent, Al Smith. Hoover was a former cabinet member, an insider who knew government was wasteful and would prosper from partnerships with large economic powerhouses. He supported the presence of powerful industrial financiers Dawes and Young inside the Congressional and Senatorial Committees to gain access to the faith and credit of the federal government. This gave insider trading a new function that has never been expunged from Congress to this day.

Within 8 months of his 1928 election, Hoover watched America stolen out from underneath the Republic by a global economic body so powerful that Congress was powerless to stop it. Everything worked exactly as planned, except for one thing. America now had an inconvenient society. The former middle class had no jobs. They had no money in the bank. They owned no property. They needed food. They needed medical care and education and they had lost their dignity. The nation did not need management. It needed leadership.

The Presidential election of Franklin D. Roosevelt was overwhelming in 1932. He won his reelection in New York as governor in 1930. The catch phrase, "It's the economy, stupid," would have been famous during the campaign. The name Roosevelt was well-known, and Americans were eager for change and for relief.

There was another reason why the election went for Roosevelt than the feeling of the people. President Herbert Hoover blamed his 1932 defeat on withdrawal of support by Wall Street and the switch of Wall Street finance and influence to Franklin D. Roosevelt. He was right. But why would Wall Street shift its support away from a man who paved the way for business to enter the committees in Congress? Why would Wall Street withdraw its support from the one man who, either by design or through skillful handling of an inexperienced politician, allowed cash to rain from heaven into the unaudited pockets of the Federal Reserve and the financial cronies of Dawes and Young?

I am glad we asked that question. The banks and power brokers were not satisfied with owning the Country of Germany for the next 90 years. They wanted to own the United States of America as well. They wanted to have a steady flow of virtually unlimited cash from the American taxpayer, and they wanted to form a new class of society that was dependent upon giving them everything they wanted in exchange for a small check each month.

The election of 1932 began an era that would establish the very America that Franklin, Jefferson, and the rest of the founding fathers feared the most. The creation of the American professional voter class had begun. Roosevelt's New Deal had programs that seemed to flow from a predesigned box of ready-made solutions. His cabinet created more than a dozen new agencies, most of which are now universally known by their acronyms. Government agencies love acronyms. These agencies are more powerful than government itself. In fact, it can effectively be argued that the professional voter class has funded a new government, the real government, while our Legislative and Judicial Branches of government just sit idly by and act like temporary employees, unhappy and powerless to do anything about it.

One more thing needed to be done to make sure that no success could penetrate or hinder their control over the economy. The money traders needed to keep their cash engine in order to control the global economy, so the President unilaterally enacted the Abandonment of gold standard in 1933. His appointee to the Federal Reserve controls the money supply to the public, while being able to write virtually unlimited blank checks to the bureaucracies he alone controls. The private ownership of gold was outlawed. Cash was allowed to float to a value set by the government through what would eventually become the Federal Reserve we know today; a group of private banks in Europe formed with the glut of wealth that was trucked into their vaults by the profits of war.

Most people do not realize the extent to which the Democrats bought the votes of hundreds of millions of citizens over more than a century of graft and subterfuge. The sad pictures and film strips showing the downtrodden were used in a national and elaborate propaganda program to convince voters to make the Federal government the employer and sole benefactor for an entire generation of people. This is a short list of the new agencies that were created:[4]

---

[4] http://en.wikipedia.org/wiki/New_Deal

- Reconstruction Finance Corporation (RFC) a Hoover agency expanded under Jesse Holman Jones to make large loans to big business. Ended in 1954.
- Federal Emergency Relief Administration (FERA) a Hoover program to create unskilled jobs for relief; replaced by WPA in 1935. Some WPA programs included adult education.
- Civilian Conservation Corps (CCC), 1933–1942: employed young men to perform unskilled work in rural areas; under United States Army supervision; separate program for Native Americans
- Homeowners Loan Corporation (HOLC) helped people keep their homes, the government bought properties from the bank allowing people to pay the government instead of the banks in installments they could afford, keeping people in their homes and banks afloat.
- Tennessee Valley Authority (TVA), 1933: effort to modernize very poor region (most of Tennessee), centered on dams that generated electricity on the Tennessee River; still exists
- Agricultural Adjustment Act (AAA), 1933: raised farm prices by cutting total farm output of major crops and livestock; replaced by a new AAA because the Supreme Court ruled it unconstitutional.
- National Industrial Recovery Act (NIRA), 1933: industries set up codes to reduce unfair competition, raise wages and prices; ended 1935. The US Supreme Court ruled the NIRA unconstitutional
- Public Works Administration (PWA), 1933: built large public works projects; used private contractors (did not directly hire unemployed). Ended 1938.
- Federal Deposit Insurance Corporation (FDIC) insures bank deposits and supervises state banks; still exists
- Glass–Steagall Act regulates investment banking; repealed 1999
- Securities Act of 1933, created the SEC, 1933: codified standards for sale and purchase of stock, required awareness of investments to be accurately disclosed; still exists.
- Civil Works Administration (CWA), 1933–34: provided temporary jobs to millions of unemployed
- Indian Reorganization Act, 1934: moved away from assimilation; policy dropped
- Social Security Act (SSA), 1935: provided financial assistance to: elderly, handicapped, paid for by employee and employer payroll

contributions; required 7 years contributions, so first payouts were in 1942; still exists

- National Labor Relations Act (NLRA) / Wagner Act, 1935: set up National Labor Relations Board to supervise labor-management relations; In the 1930s, it strongly favored labor unions. Modified by the Taft-Hartley Act (1947); still exists
- Judicial Reorganization Bill, 1937: gave the President power to appoint a new Supreme Court judge for every judge 70 years or older; failed to pass Congress
- Federal Crop Insurance Corporation (FCIC), 1938: Insures crops and livestock against loss of production or revenue. Was restructured during the creation of the Risk Management Agency in 1996 but continues to exist.
- Surplus Commodities Program (1936); gives away food to poor; still exists as Food Stamp Program
- Fair Labor Standards Act 1938: established a maximum normal work week of 44 hours and a minimum wage of 40 cents/hour and outlawed most forms of child labor; still exists, hours have been lowered to 40 hours over the years.
- Rural Electrification Administration, (REA)one of the federal executive departments of the United States government charged with providing public utilities (electricity, telephone, water, sewer) to rural areas in the U.S. via public-private partnerships. still exists.
- Resettlement Administration (RA), Resettled poor tenant farmers; replaced by Farm Security Administration in 1935.

Within 5 years, the middle class had their needs seen to in whole or in part by the Federal government. The nation went back to work in record time. Many people make the argument that regions of America would not have seen benefits like electricity, roads, education, and health care for decades. The truth will never be known, because it is impossible to recreate the same situation and try it again. Many economists believe that America would have pulled out of the mire left by the military industrial complex of World War II on its own, through free market action. The value of the economy was there. The earning capacity of America was still there.

There is an even larger and more compelling argument that the formation of a dependent class, rather than a middle class, was paramount for the success of the military industrial complex. While America was a landscape in which middle class business was rendered unable to deliver its historic and innovative abilities to pull out of the ditch with free market forces, the need for soldiers and nurses and military factory workers superseded everything else. A new class of Americans had been created in less than 5 years.

While wars rage on around the globe, the middle class was stripped of its ability to succeed and supplied with everything its citizens needed in exchange for one thing; their vote. As long as Democrats were elected, the checks would keep coming to countless mailboxes across the nation and around the globe. As long as the campaign funds kept coming into the Democrat election machine, the Agencies would continue to collect taxes and fees and launder money through to those corporations who make those contributions. It has become a multi-trillion dollar war machine.

A professional voter class had become very effectively indoctrinated, bought and paid for with a federal stipend. They were perpetually emasculated from ever being successful. It has been made famous by so many politicians over the past 60 years that even if a blue dog ran for office, if it was a Democrat, it had a loyal vote. To this very day, anyone who refuses to follow orders from Democrat leadership is publicly excoriated and financially ruined. If they should happen to prosper anyway, government agencies like the IRS have been, and are currently, employed to financially destroy them.

As of the writing of this book, the IRS is being ordered by the Senate to investigate the Tea Party Political Action Committee. The Internal Revenue Service is caught in an election-year struggle between Democratic lawmakers pressing for a crackdown on nonprofit political groups and conservative organizations accusing the tax agency of conducting a politically charged witch hunt.

The pushback is likely to be just as fierce. Jay Sekulow, a conservative lawyer known more for his stands on religious freedom than for his tax work, said he is representing 16 Tea Party groups that are claiming harassment by the I.R.S., and the number is growing. He said he intended to demand an explanation from the Treasury Department on Wednesday for what he called "McCarthyism" tactics and that he would contact Republican lawmakers this week.

"This is obviously a coordinated effort by the I.R.S. to stifle these Tea Party and Tea Party-affiliated groups, and to stifle free speech activities," Mr. Sekulow said. "It's as onerous as what they did to the N.A.A.C.P. in the 1950s, and I plan to make that point." [5]

The style and volume of the interrogatories are designed to make it impossible and/or extremely expensive for that organization to continue its political campaign support. The creation of the dependent class from the once vibrant middle class is vital to the perpetuation of the economic and political support for the military industrial complex.

There are two more things that I need to discuss in this book about the military-industrial complex. You're not going to like them, but they are as true as light itself. My skills as a master statistician always get to the root cause of any problem. This one is not hard to derive, but it is heartbreaking, nonetheless.

[5] *Scrutiny of Political Nonprofits Sets Off Claim of Harassment* By JONATHAN WEISMAN New York Times Published: March 6, 2012

Wars-R-Us

The writers of the Treaty of Versailles crafted that document to accomplish one thing and one thing only. They wanted to make sure that the suppliers of weapons and the technology of war would stay in business by guaranteeing that the Third Reich would happen. In 1919, the world's largest banks and global industrialists wiped out the middle class with an engineered crash of the stock market, and invested in technology that had a single purpose; to kill people and break things. America was about to go to war for the rest of time.

It has been called the Great American generation. Young Americans were again pumped up by government propaganda, complete with popular music and fabricated heroes, to practice killing people. They were then fed into the machines of a war that were financed and facilitated by American banks and American industrialists. On July 30, 1938, in his Dearborn, Michigan office, Henry Ford proudly accepted a Nazi medal on his 75th birthday. The Grand Cross of the Order of the German Eagle is the highest award the Reich can bestow on foreigners. The medal arrived with a note of personal greetings from Adolf Hitler.[6] He was being thanked for training and mentoring the Third Reich on how to manufacture using Ford assembly line technology. Ford also designed and built the first tanks for the American army, making huge profits from both sides of the war in Europe.

Some of the primary and more famous Americans and companies that were involved with the fascist regimes of Europe are: William Randolph Hearst, Joseph Kennedy (JFK's father), Charles Lindbergh, John Rockefeller, Andrew Mellon (head of Alcoa, banker, and Secretary of Treasury), DuPont, General Motors, Standard Oil (now Exxon), Ford, ITT, Allen Dulles (later head of the CIA), Prescott Bush, National City Bank, and General Electric. All of these individuals and companies were supporters, financiers, or suppliers of the Nazi war machine.

---

[6] http://www.historum.com/american-history/28599-henry-ford-decorated-fascist.html

The German members of the Allied Committee of Experts were equally interesting. In 1924 Hjalmar Schacht was president of the Reichsbank and had taken a prominent role in organization work for the Dawes Plan; so did German banker Carl Melchior. One of the 1928 German delegates was A. Voegler of the German steel cartel Stahlwerke Vereinigte. The United States and Germany were represented by the Morgan bankers on one side and Schacht and Voegler on the other. The rise of Hitler's Germany and subsequent German rearmament was financed by the work of this small group of financial leaders. The German industrial cartels that financed the Hitler war machine were the very same members and advisors of the major banks in New York.

As described by Carroll Quigley, this system was "... nothing less than to create a world system of financial control, in private hands, able to dominate the political system of each country and the economy of the world as a whole.[12] This feudal system worked in the 1920s, as it works today, through the medium of the private central bankers in each country who control the national money supply of individual economies.

He further explains in his amazing book, *Weapons Systems and Political Stability* (pg 12):

> "Just as our ideas on the nature of security are falsified by our limited experience as Americans, so our ideas are falsified by the fact that we have experienced security in the form of public authority and the modern state. We do not easily see that the state, especially in its modern sovereign form, is a rather recent innovation in the experience of Western civilization, not over a few centuries old. But men have experienced security and insecurity throughout all human history. In all that long period, security has been associated with power relationships and is today associated with the state only because this is the dominant form which power relationships happen to take in recent times."

Now, there is a balance to be considered here. The folks down at Wars-R-Us have studied and prepared for every aspect of war except one. The absence of war. It is a matter of logic to assume that war requires enemies. This logic would be wrong. War requires weapons and the will to use them against other human beings. If there is no enemy against which to wage war, it is of no consequence. We need not weep Alexandrian tears for a lack of empires to conquer, because war and the preparation for war is the driving force behind virtually every major new technology since the bullet.

Why? Why is it that war is the conduit through which flows the money for innovation in energy, space exploration, and even immunology? The driving force is fear. It is this one concept that we need to establish in detail here in this book.

There are three aspects of fear that justify and motivate the flow of more than $1.3 trillion a year in weapons development and production in America alone. Add to that the national budgets of every country on Earth, and the number is nothing short of staggering to behold. Here are three aspects of fear.

- The fear by the people of being conquered by another people: This is typically seen as a national defense mentality. Propaganda is used by the folks down at Wars-R-Us to keep the money flowing to their complex. They explain how bad the global neighborhood is. They tell us that large nations are aiming their missiles at us, so we should have missiles aimed at them. They tell us that small countries, who cannot hope to support a uniformed soldier, will sneak a weapon into our country and commit an act of terror against us. They tell us that our own college-educated freedom fighters are a major threat against the sovereignty of the nation.
- The fear of losing national interests: I used to think there were two national interests; the defense of the Constitution, and the exclusive control of cheap oil. In the last 11 years oil has become the sole national interest. We have gone to war to protect the free

flow of oil in the public name of spreading Democracy. We will continue to go to war to secure cheap supplies of oil without depleting our own supplies.

- The fear of losing the military industrial complex: This has nothing to do with the other two fears. The ability to make the best war in the world is what establishes power. Power is the purpose of modern warfare.

Power from modern warfare is established with two types of weapons. The first type of weapon is a deadly weapon. This is usually in the form of a missile or a bullet of some kind. The second type of weapon is a shock weapon. Hardly a day goes by that we do not hear that we are not warned that cutting any funds from the military is decimating our national defense. Anything less than $3.6 billion a day for national defense is just not good enough, so they say.

History has shown us that leaders have made wise and unwise decisions of when to use which weapon. The relationship between them has been misunderstood by historians and by military leaders as a matter of fact. These weapons are complimentary, but must be used at the right time and in the right place. Missiles are weapons of destruction and death, and shock weapons are generally weapons of duress. The former can kill men. The latter can make men obey.

When I was a young boy, I remember seeing the police cruisers emblazoned with the slogan, "To protect and to serve." That slogan is no longer there. Andy of Mayberry was an ambassador of the city and inspired the law-abiding citizen. Police size and budgets were set according to population. The usual calculation was 2% of any society would behave outside the law. Even more important was the statistical reality that 80% of crime occurred at the hands of the same perpetrators repeatedly.

Still, the function and behavior of police rapidly became more militarized. Shock weapons, which can be utilized to varying degrees for enforcement, were employed by police as well as deadly weapons. Batons, pepper spray, rubber bullets, water cannons, and high-voltage tazers are the shock weapons utilized by police. Coupled with a no-questions-allowed tactic that prevented the people from protesting the approach or engagement by a police officer, the shock is being in the proximity of a police officer. The shock of seeing a municipal soldier is what makes men obey.

Now, let's cover something for clarity. The common defense outlined in the Constitution is to be provided by the federal government to the people of this country against all enemies foreign or domestic. The only body of domestic enemies that are protected specifically in that document is the body of political protest. We have the right to assemble, but that has been truncated by regulations that prevent unlawful assembly. Unlawful assembly is that which has not been approved and permitted by the State in advance. Merely announcing on a social network that you are going to assemble can get you arrested.

I watched an armored platoon of municipal soldiers march curb-to-curb in a military short stepped stomp whilst banging their batons in unison against their shields in a shock attempt to force a civil gathering to disperse. The City Councilwoman who stood in front in her business suit trying to stop the police from attacking these young students was shot in the face with a rubber bullet. She dropped in the street with blood coming from her forehead and was rushed to the hospital. The tactic worked. Everyone fled out of fear of pain. No one was killed.

Now, let's be clear about something. The United States has been through two world wars, the Viet Nam War, the Korean War, the Spanish-American war, and dozens of skirmishes around the world involving literally millions of soldiers and thousands upon thousands of pieces of military hardware. Not once has a single bomb been dropped on a single square foot of American soil. Not one single foreign uniformed soldier has ever walked a single step on American soil since the Revolutionary War. We have thus fought all wars with impunity, able to manufacture weapons unfettered by raids or shortages of any kind. For that reason we have never been defeated.

Yet, Wars-R-Us maintains a trillion-dollar annual budget and a global presence in more than 500 military installations outside the US. The most fearsome sound in the world is the sound of the B-52. Our enemies know that this is the last sound any battlefield hears. The shock value of that aircraft alone has kept our enemies at bay for more than 50 years. It was a Cold War asset that has delivered victory without challenge.

The big enemies are all gone now. Weapons systems have been enhanced by surveillance systems. There are two types of surveillance systems; the type that we employ in space to watch the Earth, and the terrestrial-based type employed to watch the local streets. They are both extremely well deployed right now. In case you are wondering if I am right, just look up and to the right the next time you drive the freeway or a city street. You'll see a single pole with a mounted camera on it. The steel panel will be large; much larger than you would expect to control a simple camera.

There are thousands of these in every city and along the freeway. There are two questions that come to mind. First, who is sitting in front of these cameras watching? Second, what are they doing with the information? I have seen hundreds of these cameras in a single day all over town. The only way we know how effective this civilian surveillance system has become, is by watching the British police use them.

When there is a violent act in London, like a bomb going off, review experts go to the digital storage bank and find everyone who has gone into that facility in the last 24 hours. They track every single one of those people back to the point of origin and send an officer over there. Within a few hours, they have the apartment where the bomb was made, and have arrested all the people who have gone into or out of that apartment.

The same system is being constructed in America. Have you seen anyone putting these system into place along your highways? Do you know what company builds the equipment? Do you know how much the system costs, or how much of your property tax goes to pay for it? Do you know that the system is capable of checking and tracking license plate numbers, cross-checking it with the type of vehicle, and then cross checking both of those to your facial features? Do you think that it there to prevent identity theft? Do you think the government is trying to keep you safe?

The DV Master **DM-CO 2002LPH** is an intelligent vehicle license plate reading box camera featuring a built-in CAR-DC Iris Control technology which allows the camera to achieve reliable car license plate recognition for roads surveillance of a car at speeds up to 90mph.

Burns & McDonnell completed design of a comprehensive surveillance camera system for the Illinois Department of Transportation. The system involved the installation of several pole mounted CCTV cameras at strategic locations on the Dan Ryan/Stevenson interchange and the Dan Ryan/Eisenhower interchange to monitor the on and off ramps for traffic blockage.

Camera video signals transmit to a traffic system center at Oak Park, then via microwave link to IDOT District One Headquarters in Schaumberg, and finally to the Chicago-Traffic Information Center. The entire system is monitored at all three locations. Burns & McDonnell completed the project design in less than two months with extensive coordination between agencies and suppliers.

The Department of Transportation has launched the Intelligent Transportation System Exploratory Research program, intended to provide an avenue to solicit creative ideas for new technology options that are deserving of further attention and that further the ITS Strategic Research Plan goals for the next five years. The technology is rising to the challenge and to meet the grant money that has been allocated for this program.

There have been numerous, billion-dollar Initiatives enacted, funded, and completed over the past 10 years.

Current Federal ITS research programs are capitalizing on successful research initiatives initiated in 2004
Clarus - The Clarus Initiative explored ways to integrate a wide variety of weather observing, forecasting, and data management systems, combined with robust and continuous data quality checking, into systems that could deliver timely, accurate, and reliable weather and road condition information.

Congestion Initiative - The Congestion Initiative program encouraged metropolitan areas to implement the use of four complementary and synergistic strategies that contribute to the relief of urban congestion: Tolling, Transit, Telecommuting, and Technology.

Cooperative Intersection Collision Avoidance Systems (CICAS) - CICAS was a four-year program partnership between the USDOT, automobile manufacturers and State and local departments of transportation to develop vehicle-infrastructure cooperative systems that address intersection crash problems related to stop sign violations, traffic signal violations, stop sign movements and unprotected signalized left turn movements.

Electronic Freight Management - The Electronic Freight Management (EFM) initiative applied Web technologies that improved data and message transmissions between supply chain partners. It promoted and evaluated innovative e-business concepts, enabling process coordination and information sharing for supply chain freight partners through public-private collaboration.

Emergency Transportation Operations (ETO) - The ETO Initiative was a collective effort among Federal Highway Administration (FHWA), National Highway Traffic Safety Administration (NHTSA) and Federal Transit Administration (FTA). This collaborative effort encompassed six functional areas: public access to emergency services, enhanced information sharing, evacuation management and operations, transportation operations during biohazard situations, preparedness and response, and planned special events.

Integrated Corridor Management - Through the Integrated Corridor Management Systems initiative, the USDOT provided guidance to assist agencies to manage the transportation as a system—rather than the more traditional approach of managing individual assets. Agencies learned how to manage their corridor as an integrated asset in order to improve travel time reliability and predictability, help manage congestion and empower travelers through better information and more choices.

Integrated Vehicle-Based Safety Systems (IVBSS) - Through the Integrated Vehicle-Based Safety Systems (IVBSS) Initiative, the U.S. DOT established a partnership with the automotive and commercial vehicle industries to develop and field test an integrated safety system on light vehicles and commercial trucks.

41

Mobility Services for All Americans (MSAA) - Many Americans have difficulty accessing some of their basic needs because they must rely on transportation services provided for seniors, persons with disabilities and the economically disadvantaged which are often fragmented, unreliable and inefficiently operated. Lack of coordination is th leading obstacle to meeting the mobility needs of the people who need the services most. The goal of the Mobility Services for All Americans (MSAA) initiative was to improve transportation services and simplify access to employment, healthcare, education and other community activities by means of ITS technology.

Rural Safety Initiative - The goal of the Rural Safety Innovation Program was to improve rural road safety by assisting rural communities in addressing highway safety problems, heightening awareness and interest in rural safety issues, and promoting the benefits of rural safety countermeasures that could reduce rural crashes and fatalities.[7]

The Intelligent Distributed Surveillance System has been designed to provide the ability to recognize objects and humans, to describe their actions and interactions from information acquired by sensors is essential for automated visual surveillance. The increasing need for intelligent visual surveillance in commercial, law enforcement and military applications makes automated visual surveillance systems one of the main current application domains in computer vision. The emphasis of this review is on discussion of the creation of intelligent distributed automated surveillance systems. The survey concludes with a discussion of possible future directions.[8]

There is a flow for this horrendous flow of information to create a semi-automatic method for analysis. This means that thousands of video feeds don't require thousands of humans watching those screens. The software, hardware, and firmware are being upgraded in a flurrying process of capability, designed to accomplish this goal.

---

[7] http://www.its.dot.gov/res_successes.htm
[8] *Intelligent Distributed Surveillance Systems:* A review by M. Valera and S.A. Velastin (abstract) IEE Proc.-Vis. Image Signal Process., Vol. 152, No. 2, April 2005 Page 192.

Here is the traditional flow of data:

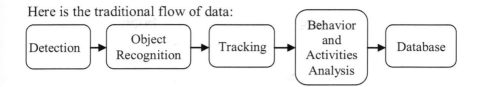

If you want to know how sophisticated and how fast this process can work, go purchase an X-Box Kinect™ and play a game without a controller. The high-speed software and the imaging system can utilize your body, compare it to the static background, and then match your behavior to actions required in the game. This game is a direct result of technology transfer activities between research companies and private corporations. The same thing is occurring with government funding.

The American bureaucracies are utilizing the IDSS just as it would any weapons system. They are using it for threat assessment.

Benjamin Franklin once said, "If the people trade Liberty for Security, they will soon have neither."

Well, it has already reached the point where the folks down at Wars-R-Us have just about everything they need to accomplish the next level of Security. In the United States federal judicial system, a single court operates in almost total secrecy, its deliberations and even its decisions are closed to the public. Created in 1978, the eleven judges of the U.S. Foreign Intelligence Surveillance Court (FIS) consider and rule on applications by federal law enforcement and intelligence agencies to conduct electronic surveillance anywhere within the United States.

The FIS Court operates under the Foreign Intelligence Surveillance Act (FISA), which regulates the gathering of foreign intelligence information inside the United States, and rarely refuses a government request to conduct special surveillance.

Section 1802(b) of the FISA authorizes the federal government to file applications for electronic surveillance with the FIS Court, and empowers

43

the FIS Court to grant orders "approving electronic surveillance of a foreign power or agent of a foreign power for the purpose of obtaining foreign intelligence information."[9]

In July 2008, Congress passed revisions to the Foreign Intelligence Surveillance Act (FISA) allowing presidential administrations to expand its foreign intelligence operations in a manner that could violate U.S. civil liberties. The Amendment was created by the president to remove the backlog of surveillance requests. In other words, a semi-automatic program designed to provide lightning-fast threat assessment and asset deployment alerts would be facilitated.

While the FISA Amendments Act specifies that no intentional surveillance of conversations between and among "United States persons" (persons resident in the United States or U.S. citizens resident in other countries), or surveillance targeting United States persons, it is very easy to imagine that the federal government would use information about U.S. persons "accidentally" obtained under FISA to target political enemies, dissidents, suspected undocumented immigrants, and suspected drug users or dealers.[10]

One of the keys to success for any security plan that is designed to prevent outside change, is to match any threat to the organization being protected. The main reason America has only come close to losing one foreign war is plain to see. Which foreign war? The Revolutionary War. Why? That is the right question.

In the Revolutionary War, America had the presence of foreign soldiers and fought battles against them on American soil. In all other wars, not a single soldier, nor a single weapon was deployed on American soil. Factories produced weapons and supplies unfettered throughout all the

---

[9] *FIS: The Nation's Secret Court A "uniquely non-public court"* by Robert Longley

[10] *The FISA Amendments Act of 2008 (H.R. 6304) What All the Fuss is About* by Tom Head

conflicts. There were no tanks rolling down neighborhood streets. There were no blackouts to prevent targeting by foreign bombers. Little more than Andy of Mayberry was required to keep the peace in America.

America will never deploy the US military to fight a domestic enemy. Americans would never allow it. We would not vote such a thing into action. There are also more guns in America than there are people, and this is precisely and specifically protected under Article 2 of the Constitution. Of course, there is no mention of ammunition. I'll cover that later.

The keys to success for the plan is early assessment and the element of surprise. Remember I said that no weapon system has ever been developed that has not been deployed? Well, the Intelligent Surveillance program was a natural option that came out of the computer industry. Smart people need grants, especially when it comes to academics. Grants from government agencies.

Government agencies have their own system of legislation and the ability to make full use of the judicial system. This is a comprehensive system that operates completely outside the purview of Congress. That's right. Congress has oversight, but is not involved in the writing, vetting, or approval of regulations written by agencies. All of these regulations have the force of law. This is a clear violation of the Constitution, but no one is even beginning to talk about curtailing it. Hundreds of thousands of attorneys and enforcement officers are funded and commanded by these agencies without any comparison to the Constitution.

These grants are at the headwaters of all weapons systems. The American surveillance system is funded, developed, deployed, continuously improved, and operated by unelected agencies that are headed by only one person; the president. With such absolute power, it is only a matter of time before the wrong person gets into that office.

This was foreseen by the founding fathers. It was absolutely their intention and design to prevent this America from becoming a reality. They knew and tried their absolute best to draft and ratify a form of government that would prevent one man from being in command of the liberty of every person in America. That power has been seized. It has been funded. In less than 10 years, it has created an infrastructure so massive and so powerful that it may never be stopped. I suppose the real question is, "Have We the People happily abdicated our liberty in totality in exchange for security?"

The USA PATRIOT Act was passed by the United States Congress in 2001 as a response to the September 11, 2001 attacks. It has ten titles, each containing numerous sections. Title II: Enhanced Surveillance Procedures granted increased powers of surveillance to various government agencies and bodies. This title has 25 sections, with one of the sections (section 224) containing a sunset clause which sets an expiration date.

The history of governmental agencies has proven one irrefutable observation. Once a power is assumed by a government, it is never released. The Patriot Act is apparently necessary in fighting the War on Terrorism. The Patriot Act expanded the Foreign Intelligence Surveillance Act of 1978 and its provisions in 18 U.S.C., dealing with "Crimes and Criminal Procedure". It also amended the Electronic Communications Privacy Act of 1986. In general, the Title expanded federal agencies' powers in intercepting, sharing, and using private telecommunications, especially electronic communications, along with a focus on criminal investigations by updating the rules that govern computer crime investigations. And those agencies write their own regulations, which have the force of law.

The folks down at Wars-R-Us needed a new agency to coordinate the surveillance of America to determine if a crime is being committed. The activities of people inside America can be determined to be a crime real time, retroactively, and without due process. In other words, any person can be tracked down to the point at which the activity was determined to be criminal through electronic means. Ignorance of the law, or regulation, is no excuse. The right to face one's accuser is not possible. One cannot cross-examine a computer.

That new agency was the Department of Homeland Security. The head of the Agency is not elected. The head of the Agency only has one commander; the president. Where is Franklin now?

> *"The Department of Homeland Security will lead the unified national effort to secure America. We will prevent and deter terrorist attacks and protect against and respond to threats and hazards to the nation. We will ensure safe and secure borders, welcome lawful immigrants and visitors and promote the free-flow of commerce."*[11]

Is this a powerful statement with numerous unconstitutional ramifications, or is this the ultimate implementation of the protection of America from enemies, both foreign and domestic? Is the DHS a master organization, unilaterally commanding other agencies, each with their own budgets, regulations, enforcement officers, and judicial processes? The answer is unequivocally, yes.

The budget for the DHS for 2013 is a whopping $59 billion, with more than 82% of it being *discretionary*!! To continue to address these *evolving threats*, the DHS employs risk-based, intelligence-driven operations to prevent terrorist attacks. Through a multi-layered detection system focusing on enhanced targeting and information sharing, DHS works to interdict threats and dangerous people at the earliest point possible. DHS also works closely with its Federal, State and local law enforcement partners on a wide range of critical homeland security issues in order to provide those on the frontlines with the tools they need to address threats in their communities. (emphasis added)[12]

When the attacks of September 11, 2001 occurred, the plan was a complete success. America was changed forever. Liberty was replaced with efforts to increase security by popular demand. Well, perhaps I should say that it

---

[11] DEPARTMENT OF HOMELAND SECURITY: Mission Statement in the *2013 Budget in Brief.* Page 10
[12] Et al page 14

was accepted without much more than a Libertarian effort to keep the bobber from being taken beneath the surface by the American people.

The military is now woven into local law enforcement like razor wire. The Federal Emergency Management Agency improved its mission to support our citizens and first responders to ensure that as a nation we work together to build, sustain, and improve our capability to prepare for, protect against, respond to, recover from, and mitigate all hazards.

The Transportation Safety Administration was formed with the mission statement:

> "We are your neighbors, friends and relatives. We are 50,000 security officers, inspectors, directors, air marshals and managers who protect the nation's transportation systems so you and your family can travel safely. We look for bombs at checkpoints in airports, we inspect rail cars, we patrol subways with our law enforcement partners, and we work to make all modes of transportation safe.
>
> The Transportation Security Administration protects the Nation's transportation systems to ensure freedom of movement for people and commerce."[13]

It sounds innocuous. The claim is to ensure freedom of movement by restricting the free movement of people and commerce. The act of searching people, luggage, packages, containers, and documents prior to letting them on aircraft is the closest thing to a police state that a nation can get without using force. Millions of travelers voluntarily waive their 4th Amendment rights by being searched without probably cause.

The **Fourth Amendment (Amendment IV)** to the United States Constitution is the part of the Bill of Rights which guards against unreasonable searches and seizures, along with requiring any warrant to be judicially sanctioned and supported by probable cause. It was adopted as a

---

[13] http://www.tsa.gov/who_we_are/index.shtm

response to the abuse of the writ of assistance, which is a type of general search warrant, in the American Revolution. Search and arrest should be limited in scope according to specific information supplied to the issuing court, usually by a law enforcement officer, who has sworn by it.

The term *unreasonable* is the adjective that has been redefined by the Executive Branch to the Judicial Branch and emasculated by the Legislative Branch. The founding fathers knew exactly what they were doing when they drafted this Amendment. They had been through it before with many monarchs over many centuries that used the violation of this individual sovereignty to eliminate their political enemies.

The entire Administration operates on regulations that have the force of law without any effective Supreme Court challenge and without any representation in the Republic. Refusing to successfully profile travelers, this one agency has affected the tone of security more than any other agency. Whoever executed the attacks of 9/11, accomplished their goal 100% with the establishment of the TSA. It is highly doubtful that Americans will ever recover their airports, bus depots, train stations, and public highways from this paramilitary organization. We have truly become one nation under surveillance. It is run directly by the President without any due process through an appointed Secretary of Homeland Security. Currently, that person is Janet Napolitano.

The rule of law has become the law of rule. The citizenry being targeted by the volumes of regulations being written every day will change as the threat evolves. The founding fathers knew that the citizen would become a threat to the president's rule. It is precisely why the Constitution gave the people the power over government, and not the other way around.

American citizens who wish to take to the streets to protest and speak out against government activities or policies are the threat. That threat may be an individual *inciting* others to taking action. That threat may be the citizens who marches with signs, or post a text on their phone or to an online social network. Each day, the police move the protestors further and further from the doors of government buildings that house the agencies to which they wish to speak.

That act of protesting against government and government agencies is the specific type of speech that is targeted for protection by the Constitution. This speech has evolved into the threat that government is trying to stop. This threat may be a comment made on a radio program or a television program. The target has become the American who believes he is no longer free. The entire $59 billion DHS program is designed to predict when that belief will turn into action, and to instantly process that action into incarceration or termination.

I suppose it is all fine, as long as we elect good men to the office of the president. I suppose if you are doing nothing wrong, you have nothing to fear. At least we can still elect the nation's leadership. I suppose.

The Occuparty

Not many people these days are unfamiliar with the Occupy Movement. I use term loosely, because this is a leaderless theater providing a platform for a large variety of protesters. When I interviewed average people about this movement, I got all kinds of responses. Some people call them the great unwashed. Some people say they are freeloaders who have never had a job and will never contain productive members of society. Some say they are socialists or criminals.

Here is my take, after all the research I have done. There is a phenomenon that occurs in sociological energy called contagion. It is a point at which a crowd suddenly changes its behavior. It has been studied posthumously for centuries. That is to say, after the smoke clears, experts went back and tried to discover the tipping point that caused the change in behavior. Experts study this for a variety of reasons, and they are significant, so I want to offer my observation.

Marketing is a profession that is dedicated to changing people's behavior. It utilizes many media such as music, testimonials, association, and of course propaganda and generally relies upon social impulse to achieve its objective. Products, for instance, are introduced a number of times in different formats and for some unknown reason one of them becomes a sensation. It is not always the best or most predictable format.

Case in point. Two forms of video recording tape format were introduced to the public as a consumer electronics product. The first was BetaMax, and the second was VHS. BetaMax was vastly superior in video bandwidth and sound quality and was American made. It was clean and common to the professional recording industry. VHS, however, was marketed in a different way. Tens of thousands of movies and millions of recorders were produced with an open architecture and were introduced by Japanese suppliers. Within a few years the results were in. VHS was a hit, and BetaMax became extinct.

Another example is the automotive world. Many hundreds of car and truck models have been designed and mass-produced. Although the brightest geniuses in marketing history are employed, and the finest design engineers the world has ever known are encouraged to dream up these models, no one knows why certain models are successful and others sit in the showrooms.

The most interesting observation is that the customers themselves do not know why they like one vehicle over another. The design process has reached a point of equilibrium. The average person cannot tell the difference between an Audi or a Toyota or a Chevy from 100 feet away. Auto makers who want to recover market share have done the only thing they can. They have reintroduced a modern version of a vintage automobile that mysteriously was a hit when it was introduced 30, 40, and even 50 years ago. The Mustang, the Challenger (note the 'Cuda was far more popular but Plymouth went out of business), the Thunderbird, and the Anglia were produced in modern versions to a second overnight success.

Yes, the Anglia. The Anglia was a car introduced in 1939 by Ford. It only sold 55 thousand units, but only because wartime demands prevented its mass production. It was fabulously famous. The modern version of this body style was an instant success. It was called the PT Cruiser and was a Chrysler that sold for an average of 20% more than the sticker price for nearly two years, even though it was a low-performance 4-cylinder automobile. Many millions of the PT Cruiser vehicles were produced in Mexico and sold in America and Europe. To this day, no one can explain why this body style was so popular until production ended in 2010.

The reason I bring this to your attention is because the auto industry is not the only organization that tries to understand what people will support with their money. Politicians also try to get the people to support their election. The definition of *politics* is the activities associated with the governance of a country or area. The connotation is something quite different. Since the very beginning of socially supported government, the people who seek power over others have no more idea of how people will vote than car makers have over which body style will be popular. So they do what the car makers cannot do. They buy votes.

One record in Kentucky probably tells it the best:

> "The lobbies, the localism, and the expectation of rewards for votes—all created an atmosphere that tacitly accepted or condoned corruption in the voting booth. In 1879 a minister visited a Simpson County canvass and told his diary: 'Oh the rabble...men aspiring to high offices treating to whiskey and buying up votes.' Vote buying, said one observer, 'is as common as buying groceries.' Even after secret ballots were implemented in 1888, problems continued to grow. One 1909 estimate indicated that up to one-fourth of all votes in the average Kentucky county could be purchased."[14]

Politics has been corrupted since men began representing other men in commerce. The honor and privilege of representing the community in government is very quickly overcome with the inflated ego of the one elected. Reelection itself becomes the focus of the person holding the office. It is as natural as any monarch accepting his life of publicity and duty along with the rights and accolades. It is, however, almost never entirely accolades. Public servants are envied and disliked by almost everyone, including those who are part of the vassaldom.

You would think that the businessman who is elected into office and suddenly cannot go to the grocery without being attacked, or who has his immediate family placed under secret service protection at all times, for the rest of their lives, would get out of politics at the earliest possible opportunity. You would think that privacy and freedom are the most valuable commodities of human existence. That assumption, apparently is false, for men seek to perpetuate their station well beyond the point at which their welcome has become thoroughly threadbare.

---

[14] *A new history of Kentucky* By Lowell Hayes Harrison, James C. Klotter Page 45.

This is vital to understanding the alienation of this nation, because the politician will do whatever it takes, including buy votes with money or whiskey, to get the voters to take action on their part. The fuse of America only took a tax on tea to become lit. The commitment to face the largest and most well funded army in the history of the world to wrest the colonies away from the very investors who funded its origination, was made after only one shot was fired. Tens of thousands of colonists lost their lives in the mayhem. The founding fathers who signed the Declaration of Independence were hunted down and destroyed almost to a man. Still, they did not give up.

When a headless, featureless, and creedless mass of Americans risk life and limb to march into batons, fists, boots, acidic pepper spray and tear gas without anyone paying them you know the energy has to be amazing. The fire in the belly began here in America.

Congressman Ron Paul supporters who held a "Boston tea-party event" in 2007 which was a fundraiser for the Ron Paul 2008 Presidential Campaign which advocated an end to fiat money and the Federal Reserve System, disengaging from foreign entanglements in Iraq and Afghanistan, and upholding States' rights.[15] Fox News commentator Juan Williams says that the TPM emerged from the ashes of Paul's 2008 presidential primary campaign.

The ashes were still warm when I travelled to Egypt in December of 2010. This was my second trip, and I was co-hosting a learning mission with my associate and friend John Riley utilizing Spirit Quest Tours. The tension was everywhere. There was a lust for extra money in the community. Everyone was targeting Americans for their tip money. John and I conducted a four-person excursion without approval from the Ministry of Antiquities to the ruins of Abu Gurab. The anomaly that lies there is the only one of its kind in the world, and a stunning feat of technology that

---

[15] Levenson, Michael (December 16, 2007). "Ron Paul raises millions in today's Boston Tea Party event". *Boston Globe*.
www.boston.com/news/local/massachusetts/articles/2007/12/16/ron_paul_raises_millions_in_todays_boston_tea_party_event/. Retrieved April 9, 2010.

remains unexplained. No tourists know about it, and barely any of the archaeologists will even attempt the trek.

Suffice it to say that it takes a good chunk of Egyptian money and a trusting cab driver to get you there. Everyone along the way must be bribed...er, uh tipped. We knew we only had about an hour to get the photos we were looking for, as the last time we had visited this site was with a larger group some years before. There was barely a footprint left on top of ours from the trip before.

We dug down in the sand with our hands, as getting caught with digging tools would have landed us in prison for sure. The light was just right, and I shot the digitals for my study when our trusted cab driver, Habib, started waiving his hands and shouting and pointing. He was telling us the police were coming.

We looked out over the sand, and there was a single man in western clothes on a small burro that was galloping for all its worth straight for us from another site 3 kilometers away, Abu Sir. We gathered up our cameras and started running for the barbed wire fence. He had not seen what we were doing. We kept the film running and ran for about 500 meters across the desert to the fence of the date grove where we had entered the desert. We arrived under the fence before he ever got to the site where we were digging. I had shoved all the sand back in place and smoothed it out to look like nothing had been accessed. It worked.

The antiquities police officer arrived at the small guard shack, where we had of course heavily bribed the barefoot attendant. He lied for us in Arabic. We had tea and smoked a Hookah filled with some horrible black weed that looked uncomfortably like manure. It was smooth and strong. The police officer had a smoke and was clearly stalling for something. Habib leaned over and in the only English he apparently knew said, "You have. You have," while rubbing his thumb and first to fingers together. We paid the officer about 600 Egyptian pounds. He smiled and told us not to go back under the fence. We smiled back.

As we arrived back in the city of Cairo later that afternoon, there was a buzz that was unlike the regular Giza glowthat everyone feels when they visit this sleepless society. On the one hand, there were less than the usual military vehicles driving through town. On the other hand, there were crowds of people gathering here and there in the market places. They were not shopping. They were talking. The blaring call to prayer around the Egyptian Museum was accompanied by what I can only describe as a southern preacher.

At first, he was telling the people in Arabic that Allah was great and would bless the people. Yes, I speak some Arabic, but Greg and Halle understand much more. Our authorized Egyptian tour guide, from whom John and I slipped away for better pictures on a regular basis, was translating as well. I was very familiar with what followed, as I have lived almost my whole life in the southern states.

He caught the *spirit* as we like to say. His voice changed. He began to get into a rhythm and a cadence that was exactly like fire and brimstone. He called for the people to reclaim their country. He asked them to have courage and not to falter. He said Allah was willing for the people to throw out the Western man. The Western man? At first, we thought this was us; you know, Americans. Our tour guide told us not to worry. It didn't mean us. Egyptians love Americans. They were talking about the leaders of Egypt.

It was true. I had been all over Egypt from North to South. I had ridden for days on busses through the countryside and into all of the major cities. It was the same wherever we went. The canals, fed by the Nile and dug hundreds of years before to bring water to the villages and suburbs of the cities, were choked with trash and waste. Along the sides of the canals there would be gasoline-powered water pumps that would pump the water like a fire hydrant up the bank to catch basins the people would bring to fill. It was their drinking water. It was water for bathing. It was also filled with death, disease, trash, and pollution. It had not changed at all from the time I visited before.

In addition, there was an ancient cemetery in Cairo. Egyptians treat death differently that Western cultures. They visit the dead and stay for about 30 days to mourn and reminisce. Tombs have provisions for this with rooms and stone tables for preparing sacrifices and meals and for sleeping. It is a veritable town within the City. It is also occupied by more than one million people who live there.

There is no water, no sewer, and no electricity. It is a City of the dead. There is a subculture of young people throughout Egypt who see what has happened to their country. It was neglected and obfuscated by its president. For more than 30 years, Mubarak had taken hundreds of billions of dollars and built for himself and his family the wealth of kings with holdings in nearly every major country. His people did not have a clean glass of water. To this day, there is not a single traffic light in the entire city of Cairo with more than 20 million people.

Inspired by the Tea Party of America, and utilizing the hitherto innocuous social networks of Twitter and Facebook, the youth began to plan. The preacher of Cairo blaring his call to action over the loudspeakers of Tahrir Square. On January 17, 2011, just a couple of months after we left Egypt, the most sought-after event in history occurred. Millions of young people spilled into Tahrir Square demanding the resignation of Hosni Mubarak.

There were four factions who had power. The military was aligned with itself. Once taking orders from the President, they had the bullets and the equipment. The leadership was as frustrated with Mubarak's greed and wanted to take over the country for a long time. They saw this as their opportunity.

The police were really nothing more than henchmen for Mubarak. They were the ones who beat people to death in the streets and staged violence to blame on the peaceful protesters. They dressed like protesters and set fires and threw stones and looted stores. The Western press bought the ruse without question. I know this for a fact, because one of my friends was there sitting on the curb of Tahrir Square when it happened and witnessed it first-hand.

The people were anonymous. Just like their Libertarian associates in America, and like their forefathers before them, they were throwing the tea into the harbor. They wanted the leadership to leave. They did not have a plan for replacement. There was no charismatic leader pumping them up. They surged as a people with one mind and one heart. They only wanted Democracy, and they didn't understand the step after Anarchy.

The Muslim Brotherhood understood the step after Anarchy very well. They are well-funded and organized. They have Islamic government in a box, dehydrated. All you have to do is add blood, and you have a government. They moved in to fill the vacuum and ran into the other group that already had its feet propped up on the desks of their previous owners. The military had already seized control in the name of the people, and would keep the peace until government could be reorganized. It has been over a year, and not a single thing has changed. The people are ready to once again take up their shoes. Placing a shoe upon the face or effigy of an enemy is equivalent to dusting off one's shoes on someone in the Christian culture. It means the wrath of God is called down upon you. No one does this, or takes this lightly.

During the year since the Egyptian ejection of Mubarak, the energy has come full circle back to America. The American Tea Party was formed by the Libertarians and had summarily been hijacked by the Republicans, the same as in Egypt. The parting on the Right, became the Parting on the Left as Roger Daltry would sing. Nothing changed. The energy was absorbed and warmed the water in the giant hot tub of Congress for a while. Another buzz word or two was added to the political Lexicon. Nothing more.

Now, the second cycle is beginning. In the Fall of 2011, less than a year after what the press calls the Arab Spring, the young people began taking to the streets of America. Of course, we are numbed by million-man this and million-man that in Washington. Every face was photographed and every speaker was placed on one list or another for special investigation. The grass was mowed, and the litter was cleared away, and the cameras were shelved, and no one cares as ten million people flood the Mall in

Washington. The President would go to Hawaii or to Martha's Vineyard and other leaders would use the back exit to Congress for their safety.

The energy of Liberty is one that will never die. Although its seekers may have their faces broken by paramilitary police who are just following orders, they will not stop seeking. University of California at Davis students silently sitting in protest to alert their fellow alumni that liberty has been traded for security had their faces casually and methodically filled with pepper spray as the cameras were rolling. Their American pride is now joined in their dreams with their screams of agony as they are publicly tortured for the world to see.

At a news conference, University President Katehi said what the video shows is, "sad and really very inappropriate" but defended her leadership and said she had no plans to resign.
"I do not think that I have violated the policies of the institution," she said. "I have worked personally very hard to make this campus a safe campus for all."

The police called it standard procedure. Katehi remained in a media room for more than two hours after the news conference, eventually walking to an SUV past a group of students nearly three blocks long who, in a coordinated effort, remained completely silent. Hundreds and hundreds of students lined the sidewalk on both sides as President Katehi made her way to her waiting SUV. The sound of her heels on the sidewalk was the only sound. The staring eyes of the students were louder than any gun. They were more powerful than any document. The nation will never forget. It was the silence heard around the world.

Every major city in America has a group of Americans who are expressing this energy. Many of them are smart and intelligent—yes there is a difference—and they are learning about the Constitution and the passion the founding fathers had when they crafted it. It was written for them. The authority is there. The will to sacrifice is what it takes. Freedom, after all, isn't free at all.

Winning any political fight requires popularity. Mass media has made its living creating and destroying popularity. It doesn't matter to them. Either one sells commercials. While the protesters who take to the streets try to get noticed by the cameras, the commentators are interpreting for the television audience. If you will remember, while the video of millions of young people holding hands and singing standing together in Tahrir Square in Cairo showed live on the screen behind her, the news commentator ranted about how the government was going to stop the violence by the protestors. What violence? Did she mean the bones that were broken by police jeeps as they ran over innocent unarmed people who could not get out of the way? Did she mean the mobs who were beaten with batons and stomped by horses as Mubarak tried to keep his seat of power? That violence? No. She was telling her viewers that the protesters were violent, and the police were merely defending themselves and trying to restore law and order. You now know she was lying.

You can go ahead and finish your popcorn in the safety of your living room, because that violence is in Cairo or in Syria and not in your neighborhood. You do not have a memory of tanks rolling down your street, or the sounds of gunfire into a crowd of people. You have never felt the building shake as rockets sent by someone following orders fall during the night. You have never even heard aircraft other than at the airport, and you wouldn't remember the growl of guns vomiting death to the streets below. That is over there. It isn't here. Yet.

The Occuparty is not a mass of unwashed freeloaders who want to take what the rich have accumulated from their own hard work. Each of them aspires to such success. But the opportunity to make it does not exist for them. It never will. The bridges to that side of the chasm have been removed or are heavily guarded by those on the other side. There is no infrastructure that facilitates the ambition that made this country what it is today.

Small business access to capital no longer exists, because the agency-government has borrowed every last dollar that will be printed for the next 20 years and spent it on growing itself even larger. We the people helplessly watch as unspeakably large dollar amounts are passed from the taxpayer to criminals and cohorts who claim they have no idea where all that money went. Millions, billions and trillions of dollars pour through the laundry so fast that no one dares even put their hand into the stream of greed.

Members of the Occuparty see this ocean of money crashing upon the luxury beaches of the largest corporations in the world, and they are mad about it. American students have to pay hundreds of thousands of dollars to gain skills while foreign students fill our universities funded by endless fountains of cash sent with them by their third-world governments. The argument can be made that foreign students that come to America for an education are the best of the best. Their governments pay the way, even at highly inflated tuitions, because it is an investment in their own national future. Likewise, American students with top grades can get a college education paid for by scholarships and grants. Only the students with average academic achievements have to actually pay for their education. The conclusion is that the student faction of the Occuparty is made of average students without scholarships. If they got better grades, they would pay nothing for an education. Still, they are voting Americans who see a massive disparity that leaves them in the ditch while the wealthy receive all the assistance.

Hundreds of thousands of small business loan applications sit unprocessed in government offices all over the country. In the mean time, hundreds of billions of dollars in grants, loans, and loan guarantees are silently passed to the world's largest and wealthiest corporations, like GE, GM, Disney, and Toyota while the most incredible energy and transportation technologies the world has ever seen gathers dust in garages, basements, and small shops all over America. Among the most common arguments made by Occuparty spokespeople is that the mega-corporations can cover the costs of their own R&D. Why is the American taxpayer giving them anything? It is the small business owner and innovator that needs that taxpayer support to enter the market and offer alternatives to oil as a fuel for transportation or for powering a home or business.

True Libertarians, that made up the core energy of the Tea Party before it was hijacked by the Republicans, make the valid claim that the taxpayer funds should never have left the person who worked for them in the first place. The Federal government is not specifically empowered by the Constitution to redistribute wealth, and thus they should cease and desist. The taxpayer has the right to do with their money whatever they want including spend it all. Of course, this would mean that there would be no treasury and no ability for the public to vote a piece of it for itself.

The Occuparty sees something the press does not see. They see that the agency-government is nude. Oh, the agencies say they have clothes, and the denigration will be limitless you do not agree with them. The Occuparty sees their bleached asses jiggling down the sidewalks of Wall Street and that no one but them is saying anything about it. They see the players in this massive shell game move from agency to business to public office and back to agency. The founding fathers saw the President as the monarch of America, and the leader of the world. They knew that too much power in the hands of one man could be awesome in the right person, and tyranny if not.

When tyranny rises out of the ashes of man's greed, the energy of the Occuparty will not be far behind as long as the spirit of America lives. As you read this book, you are feeling the same fire inside of you. You do not have to look down at a set of numbers tattooed on your arm to know this. You do not have to watch a movie about how tens of millions of people willingly march through inspection lines and willingly offer their most private financial secrets to government officers. You do not have to read a history book to know what it is like to see every dollar earned by the people seized by a government and redistributed without your advice or consent.

You know what, "See something, say something," sounds like. Your neighbors are watching you. Cameras are watching you. You have already watched the protesters of the Occuparty, in the face of tyranny, willing to go out in the streets and take the beating and the gassing and the torture in the name of liberty. You don't have to do anything. You can sit here and read this book and watch the news, and you don't have to say or do a thing. The protesters will speak for liberty with their feet.

Yes, liberty is messy and unorganized and impoverished and sometimes jumps off the branch before its feathers are fully formed. The time will soon come, as long as it does not give up or lose faith or listen to the popcorn crunchers drunk with agency propaganda, that it will take flight. It will become the eagle again and carry the flag of liberty skyward over smoky ramparts to set the people free.

History tells us that once the grip of the agency-government is broken, the most powerful players move in to seize control of the cash and the power. The Tea Party has already been hijacked. The Occuparty wrestling match is total anarchy right now as various factions fight for the controlling voice. They are all alienated from America, but they are also alienated from one another. A mini-republic is forming among the cyber-community with flash mobs cocked and ready to pounce on one issue or another. Like dozens of third-world struggles around the world, this tumor Republic has no leader and no platform and no solutions. Protesting has to have a point. The entire world is waiting for them to get to the point.

So when I talk about the messy energy of liberty, have some hope that the presence of the energy itself is a symptom of the disease of tyranny. The reason I write this book is that the media spends all its time covering the symptom and has completely neglected the disease. Any time the citizens allow government to grow itself, without the representation of those citizens, the Occuparty energy will appear and grow in protest to match it.

That is the beauty of a Republic. The citizens elect representatives to go to Washington to tell their point of view and vote to benefit that community. When the elected person does not do that job satisfactorily, they are fired and someone else is sent to do it. Term limits are swift and democratic. Sounds simple.

When that process does not work, that is to say when no matter who the citizens send to Washington the same problems persist, then the citizens realize that the process is broken and must be fixed. The process is so broken now, with more than 43% of the Federal budget and nearly all the legislation being consumed by agencies that are not elected, nor are they accessible by the citizens, that citizens are gathering for the next civil war.

Hopefully, the entire conflict will take place on the battlefield of the election booth.

There is actually a movement that looks much like the same energy of the Occuparty, except they have chosen to work within the election system and seek to replace every member of Congress that does not represent his or her district. They are targeting the career politicians who have built this behemoth of a bureaucracy and receive thousands upon thousands of lobbyists and use the power of their elected office to make themselves and their friends wealthy.

The Get out of our House (GOOOH) movement is a NON-PARTISAN plan to place citizen representatives on the ballot in 2012, ideally in the primary against the incumbent, competing for a seat in the U.S. House of Representatives. The members of each district will have an honest opportunity to replace the career politicians who have taken over OUR House and are destroying our nation.

It is NOT a political party. It is a system that will allow you and your neighbors to choose, among yourselves, a candidate who will truly represent your district. Members will select a citizen representative to serve their district. How our candidates get on the ballot will be dependent on when we reach our membership goal. Our preference is to compete in the primaries against the incumbent. It is possible candidates may choose to run in some other way; the candidates will make that decision based on the situation in their district. It is important to clearly state that we are not a third party. We have no platform and are a bottom-up organization. We are a process for selecting and funding candidates.[16]

---

[16] http://goooh.com/Learn.aspx

The Silent Scream

I began studying this subject about 20 years ago when I was working on a team to elect a new Tennessee Senator. I was so moved by the statistics and the facts of this subject that I decided to get involved. Within a year I was elected to be president of the largest chapter in the State and produced excellent support for the candidate the State sent to Washington. I became a speech writer for Alan Keyes and delivered one of the speeches to multiple standing ovations at the Lincoln Birthday fundraiser in Chattanooga, Tennessee. I was also nominated to be a delegate to the 1996 presidential election, which I turned down.

Each year, about 30 thousand people die on American highways. Actually the rate of traffic fatalities have steadily fallen since 2007, in part because people are driving less and in part because a threshold of safety measures in vehicles has been reached.

About ten times that number of Americans are killed each year without ever being able to make a sound, because they don't yet breathe air. More than 30 million Americans have been denied the right to life by a single multi-billion dollar organization that operates under the guise of a women's health provider.

Don't start with me. I am pro-choice, in the sense that I believe a woman has the right to choose whether or not to become pregnant. No woman should become pregnant who does not want to be pregnant. That is not the point for the commercialization of this mega-corporation and never was. It was always about the money.

Planned Parenthood charges about $500 cash for each fetal termination. There are no terms for such a procedure, because the emotional crash after such an event is so powerful that women have a difficult time making payments for a procedure that she will spend the rest of her life trying to expunge from her memory. These procedures are always paid in advance of the actual procedure. Planned Parenthood performed 329,445 fetal terminations in 2010.

This is one of the dirty little secrets kept quiet by the large political contributions and lobby groups that operate in Washington. Planned Parenthood Federation of America (PPFA), commonly shortened to Planned Parenthood, is the U.S. affiliate of the International Planned Parenthood Federation (IPPF) and one of its larger members. PPFA claims to be a non-profit organization providing *reproductive health* and maternal and child health services. The Planned Parenthood Action Fund, Inc. (PPAF) is a related organization which lobbies for pro-choice legislation, comprehensive sex education, and access to affordable health care in the United States.

Planned Parenthood is the largest provider of what they claim are *reproductive health services* in the United States, which include contraceptives and abortions, among other services. Contraception accounts for 35% of PPFA's total services and abortions account for 3%; PPFA claims they conduct roughly 300,000 abortions each year, among 3 million people served. The actual numbers, reported by the Guttmacher Institute exceed 1.2 million abortions each year. By any standard, about 30% of the women treated by Planned Parenthood lose a living child in the process.

The organization has its roots in Brooklyn, New York, where Margaret Sanger opened the country's first birth-control clinic. Sanger founded the American Birth Control League in 1921, which in 1942 became part of the Planned Parenthood Federation of America.

Since then, Planned Parenthood has grown to over 820 clinic locations in the U.S., with a total annual budget of US $1 billion. PPFA provides an array of services to over three million people in the United States, and supports services for over one million clients outside the United States.[17]

What you are about to read is one of the most powerful points of fact in the alienation of Americans from America. On October 19, 1939, Margaret Sanger outlined a plan for stopping the growth of the Black community. She predicted in her owns words that "the most successful educational

---

[17] http://en.wikipedia.org/wiki/Planned_Parenthood

approach to the Negro is through a religious appeal. We do not want word to go out that we want to exterminate the Negro population and the minister is the man who can straighten out that idea if it ever occurs to any of their rebellious members." Her planning, which included being careful to make it appear that hand-picked Blacks are in control, has been an undeniable financial success even today. Faye Wattleton's position as President of PPFA was testimony to that fact.

The Birth Control Review, founded by Sanger in 1917, was totally committed to the eugenics philosophy. Eugenics is the study of or belief in the possibility of improving the qualities of the human species or a human population, especially by such means as discouraging reproduction by persons having genetic defects or presumed to have inheritable undesirable traits **(negative eugenics)** or encouraging reproduction by persons presumed to have inheritable desirable traits **(positive eugenics).**

The official editorial policy of The Review endorsed I.Q. testing, which classified Blacks, southern Europeans, and other immigrants as mentally inferior to native-born White Americans and called them a nuisance and a menace to society. In the 1920s she tried to use the results from I.Q. tests, which classified the U.S. soldier as a near moron, to back up her own findings.

Sanger truly believed these groups were a "dead weight of human waste" and "a menace to the race."[18]

Throughout the pages of the Birth Control Review, Mrs. Sanger's journal, there are countless quotes which not only suggest that she favored eugenics, but that she provided a forum to those who wished to spread their fear of human life, when that life was conceived by someone other than a member of society's elite.

Since 1942, the organization has grown to one of the biggest political sledgehammers in Washington. Labeled as the *freedom of choice,* or as *women's reproductive rights,* or even *women's health services,* the

---

[18] Drogin, pp. 17, 46.

leadership advertises contraception, but conducts a global business of fetal termination all the way up to the point where the child can breathe on its own.

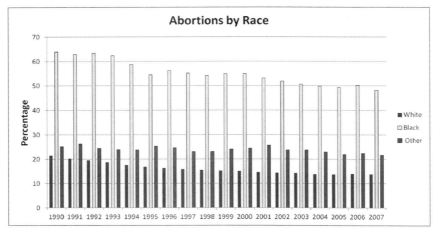

Abortions by Race

The graph shows the results of the organization's marketing plan, their physical locations in the community, and the demographics of the services. Planned Parenthood has terminated so many black children that Hispanics surpassed blacks as the largest minority in America in 2004.

Although more than 30 million fetal terminations have been performed, the planning behind the procedure is the key to why I included this information in this book. The agency-government has alienated us from our own unborn.

Rape	0.30%
Incest	0.03%
physical life of mother	0.20%
Physical health of mother	1.00%
Fetal health	0.50%
Personal Choice	97.97%

Reasons Reported for Abortions

The number to pay attention to in the table above is the Personal Choice data. All the marketing and lobbying for Planned Parenthood contains a pure focus on the first 5 reasons posted above, which as you can see total to about 2.03% of the total amount of fetal terminations. They make public and powerful efforts to never mention the last reason in any of their marketing information. It is abundantly clear that fetal termination is practiced as birth control. The question remains, "What are they trying to control?"

The personal choices are grouped together in the table, but there is a global demographic spread that is important to know about. A 2005 study estimated that over 90 million females were "missing" from the expected population in Afghanistan, Bangladesh, China, India, Pakistan, South Korea and Taiwan alone, and suggested that sex-selective abortion plays a role in this deficit. India's 2011 census shows a serious decline in the number of girls under the age of seven - activists believe eight million female fetuses may have been terminated between 2001 and 2011.

Some research suggests that culture plays a larger role than economic conditions in gender preference and sex-selective abortion, because such deviations in sex ratios do not exist in sub-Saharan Africa, Latin America, and the Caribbean. Other demographers, however, argue that perceived gender imbalances may arise from the underreporting of female births, rather than sex-selective abortion or infanticide. Sex-selective abortion was rare before the late 20th century, because of the difficulty of determining the sex of the fetus before birth, but ultrasound has made such selection easier. There is an ultrasound unit within walking distance of nearly every abortion clinic in the world. Prior to this, parents would alter family sex compositions through infanticide.[19] That is abortion after the baby is born.

In America, we call this late-term abortion. All the way up to the ninth month, significantly after any fetus could be delivered as viable through Cesarean Section, children can be killed and discarded. The procedure is performed after the head clears the vaginal opening. Just as the baby is opening its eyes to look upon its new world, the physician pierces the base of the skull, severing the connection between the brain and the body. If he is skillful, the mother will never hear the baby's first cry.

The disclosure of late-term fetal terminations shocked the American public. Planned Parenthood has effectively impoverished any politician who mentions this procedure in any public rhetoric. The termination of female babies is an anthropological phenomenon never mentioned in history. Men have been lost in war and even into bondage, but women have been preserved to protect the propagation of the human race. Females are the limiting factor to any race. What was even more shocking was that these countries were not the only ones practicing such atrocities.

A 2006 Zogby poll found that 86% of Americans support a ban on gender-based abortions. However, legislation sponsored by Congressman Trent Franks in 2009 to enact such a ban was not approved. Fortunately, Congressman Franks is not easily dissuaded, and remains committed to making this procedure illegal in America. He will be reintroducing his legislation, the Prenatal Nondiscrimination Act (PRENDA), passed out of committee as HR 3541. This legislation would ban all gender-based abortions, as well as all race-based abortions. As of the writing of this book, the legislation is not making progress toward passage. Within

---

[19] http://en.wikipedia.org/wiki/Sex-selective_abortion

minutes of the legislation coming out of committee, the Planned Parenthood press army began its work.

> "This is incredibly f---ing disturbing, but this is what we've come to: male lawmakers are attempting to pass laws that would allow a man to sue a woman for refusing to carry his child to term, or a woman's parents to file an injunction to keep their teenage daughter pregnant. But not only are lawmakers trying to write laws that would make a woman's uterus subject to the approval of her parents or partner, they're trying to do it under the guise of "civil rights." Your body, their choice."[20]

While the problem of American gender-based abortion is at first glance more obvious because how prevalent and public it is, the occurrence of race-based abortions is equally abhorrent and possibly just as common. It is particularly alarming that Planned Parenthood has been caught on camera accepting funds for the purpose of aborting minority babies. This fact alone – the largest abortion provider in the world is willing to earmark funds for the abortion of minority babies – makes it clear that race-based abortions must also be outlawed.

The American Center for Law and Justice applauds Congressman Franks for his heroic stand against race-based and gender-based abortions. [21]

The facts are beginning to make their way to the many foundations that donate money to Planned Parenthood. The proof is so stark and so offensive, that they have begun to withdraw their support. Do you think the Alienated Nation exists? Wait until you hear this story.

Breast cancer charity giant Susan G. Komen for the Cure chose not to renew a grant to Planned Parenthood to fund breast exams, under the direction their Vice-President Karen Handel. She had already publicly

---

[20] 'Prenatal Nondiscrimination Act' Is Actually Designed to Let Men Block Abortions Jezebel Magazine by Erin Gloria Ryan Feb 20, 2012

[21] *Gender and Race-Based Abortions a Problem the U.S. Must Fix:* nu Nathanael Bennett LifeNews.com 11/30/2011

stated her opposition to abortion, a service provided at most of the Planned Parenthood facilities. Handel wrote in her unsuccessful gubernatorial campaign blog that she "does not support the mission of Planned Parenthood."

"During my time as Chairman of Fulton County, there were federal and state pass-through grants that were awarded to Planned Parenthood for breast and cervical cancer screening, as well as a 'Healthy Babies Initiative,'" Handel wrote. "Since grants like these are from the state I'll eliminate them as your next Governor." She also wrote that she opposes stem cell research and supports crisis pregnancy centers, which are unregulated, Christian-run operations whose main mission is to convince pregnant women not to have abortions.

Over the five years prior to Handel's January 30th announcement, the Komen organization had given Planned Parenthood health centers the funds to provide nearly 170,000 clinical breast exams to low-income and uninsured women. She had made the statement that there was little evidence that Planned Parenthood actually provided the breast exams, and instead used the funds to pay for abortions. Pro-Choice activists claimed that Handel compromised to pressure from anti-abortion lawmakers and organizations to cut off hundreds of thousands of dollars in grants to Planned Parenthood.

By February 2nd, the lobbyists full frontal attack forced the issue to the front pages all over the world. The Susan G. Komen for the Cure foundation apologized for cutting off funding from Planned Parenthood and vowed to revise the policy that led to an intense backlash against the nation's largest breast cancer organization.

"We want to apologize to the American public for recent decisions that cast doubt upon our commitment to our mission of saving women's lives," president and founder Nancy Brinker said in a statement today. "We have been distressed at the presumption that the changes made to our funding criteria were done for political reasons or to specifically penalize Planned Parenthood. They were not.

"Our original desire was to fulfill our fiduciary duty to our donors by not funding grant applications made by organizations under investigation," she added. "We will amend the criteria to make clear that disqualifying investigations must be criminal and conclusive in nature and not political. That is what is right and fair."[22]

The next day, Karen Handel resigned.

For nearly 30 years, surveys have been done to validate the general feeling about fetal terminations in America. 86% of people, and roughly the same percentage of voters, think that abortion as a form of birth control is wrong.

"The No Taxpayer Funding for Abortion Act is non-partisan. Nearly 70 percent of Americans, pro-life and pro-choice, don't want their dollars going to pay for abortion," said Nance. "If President Obama vetoes this legislation, he will be stomping on the freedoms we hold dear in this country and making every one of us complicit in abortion, a moral abhorrence for over half of the population."[23] The rhetoric is locked and loaded by billion-dollar propagandists who have proven they are ready to politically destroy anyone who attempts to stop the flow of money and control over the demographics of society.

Still, more than $1 billion annually is laundered through other programs labeled as women's health services and provided to Planned Parenthood for legitimate health services to offset the costs of providing abortions. The effect is the same.

Several major cities worth of Americans have been silenced because of the billion-dollar abortion industry established by Margaret Sanger. It is one of the most direct examples of a mega-corporation consuming tax dollars

---

[22] *Susan G. Komen Apologizes for Cutting Off Planned Parenthood Funding* et al
[23] *Bill to ban federal abortion funding up for a vote*: by Caroline May Daily Caller May 4, 2011

to provide a service that results in the death of more than one third of its patients.

Americans and politicians have looked the other way while this industry has operated unchecked for many decades. Its operation has alienated millions of Americans from their children, their wives, and their government agencies. Karen Handel was proud to run a foundation that is dedicated to saving women's lives by winning the battle against breast cancer. She was completely dedicated to her company and was so heartbroken that the abortion bureaucracy was strong enough to force the company to reverse her decision that she resigned. That, my friends, is the ultimate alienation.

When you are full of love and hope and intelligent anticipation, but you breathe amniotic fluid instead of air, it is impossible to scream.

Sovereignty

In America, States have rights under the US constitution. These rights are those not specifically delegated to the Federal government in the Constitution. That's it. What could be more simple than that? If the Constitution doesn't specifically say that the Federal government can do something, it cannot do it.

The founding fathers believed in enmity between State and Federal power. The declaration of a State to be sovereign from the Federal government was one of the driving forces behind the Southern states declaring their independence in 1861. The 21st century State Sovereignty phenomenon clearly arises from the belief that the balance of power has tilted too far and for too long in the direction of the Federal government and that time has come to restore that balance.

The Federal government is a loose coalition between bureaucracies that compete against one another for the American checkbook. That account is filled by you, the American taxpayer. The agency-government has become so large, it even has an agency through which you must go to do business with other agencies. The General Services Administration is an organization that writes its own laws, conducts its own enforcement actions, and restricts products available to other agencies to those produced by multi-billion dollar global corporations. It is even illegal for Congress to speak to them on behalf of any small business trying to do business through the GSA.

And while the small business owner is stymied by having to conform with the agency's *capability clause*[24], that same agency spent more than $820 thousand on a Las Vegas party for its employees, all at the taxpayer's expense. As of the writing of this book, only the Secretary has been asked to resign. The rest of the 300 gluttons, who consumed more than $140 thousand in food and alcohol in three days, are invoking protection from prosecution under the 5th Amendment right against self-incrimination. You can see what a plutarchian union of criminals the agency-government

---

[24] FAR 9.104-1

has become while you were sleeping on the train. Fortunately, there are those whom citizens have elected on the State level that are trying to scrape these barnacles off the once sleek and swift hull of America.

The emergence of this movement is a hopeful sign of the people asserting their rights and the rights of the States. We the people are about to discharge the runaway Federal government. With the threat of increasingly out of control Federal spending, some of these sovereignty bills have some teeth in them. Most are civil shows of strength without any legal basis. Most of them are invitations to a battle in court.

These non-binding resolutions, often called "state sovereignty resolutions," do not carry the force of law. Instead, they are intended to be a statement of the legislature of the state that has the ability to end up in court. They play an important role, however. It is through these declarations that the People will finally be invited to the podium to speak.

If you owned an apartment building and had a tenant not paying rent, you wouldn't show up with an empty truck to kick them out without first serving notice. There is a peaceful and legal process of evicting someone from your house. That's how we view these Resolutions – as serving "notice and demand" to the Federal government to "cease and desist any and all activities outside the scope of their constitutionally-delegated powers." Follow-up, of course, is a must. A *Forcible Detainer* filing does nothing without the judgment AND the sheriff showing up to toss their belongings in the street. In the case of a delinquent Federal agency, the furniture stays. It belongs to the people who own the building.

There's a lot of excitement about these bills, but there are also a lot of misconceptions, with people claiming that some States have already declared sovereignty and that the movement is much farther along than it really is. Some States have debated, passed, and ratified their Sovereignty Acts, including establishing a State coinage and have *set aside* unfunded Federal mandates. Some have flatly refused to enforce certain Federal laws, banking that the feds don't have the manpower or the cajones to enter a State with an enforcement action. State utility providers are losing that gamble every day with the agency-government soldiers of the EPA.

Oklahoma's bill passed their lower house overwhelmingly but stalled in the Senate last fall and is being held over for consideration in the new year.

Contrary to the fantasies of some extremists, these sovereignty bills are not the first step toward secession or splitting up the union, nor are they an effort to block collection of the income tax, appealing though as that might be. For the most part, they are not so much political statements of independence as they are expressions of fiscal authority directed specifically at the growing cost of unfunded mandates being placed upon the states by the federal government. Despite the movement picking up steam as he came to office, the target of these bills is not President Obama, but rather the Democrat-dominated Congress whose plans for massive bailouts and expanded social programs levy enormous costs on the states.

Within a few decades of the Revolutionary War ending in 1787, the Federal government began to grow on its own in ways that demanded more and more resources from the States, although without benefits to the States from which the revenues were taken. This prompted the State legislatures to pass a series of acts of sovereignty called the Nullification Acts. Nullification is a legal theory that a U.S. State has the right to nullify, or invalidate, any federal law that a state has deemed unconstitutional or unenforceable by the State. The action by the legislatures actually set aside—a legal term meaning to take no action at this time—new Federal laws until they were ratified by the State. In some cases, the law was never ratified, which nullified the authority over the country as a whole. The agency-government utilizes regulations with the force of law, showing no fear nor respect of the State authorities.

The current state movements toward Sovereignty Acts are approaching the Nullification Crisis of 1832 where the State of South Carolina asserted that it had the right to nullify the authority of federal laws within its borders. It was only the leader. Eloquent and impassioned pleas in the halls of Congress for relief from Federal tyranny over Southern States, drew twelve States to her side. The current movement is just outside the broad Doctrine of Nullification, reasserting the limits which the 10th Amendment places on federal authority. As of the writing of this book, at least 40 States have passed or are in the process of passing sovereignty Acts, effectively nullifying certain Federal laws inside those States. Most directly, this legal stance is being taken on what are termed unfunded Mandates by the Federal government. The agency-government is a different animal. These agencies have teeth, and they have shown no hesitation at enforcement actions.

Not all of the bills fall within these limitations. Missouri's bill actually goes somewhat further and asserts the right of the State to negate federal law, specifically in reference to the proposed federal Freedom of Choice Act, which some fear would bar states from passing laws regulating abortion. [25]

New Hampshire's bill actually goes so far as to lay out a very strongly worded variant of the Doctrine of Nullification which specifies acts by the Federal government which would effectively negate the authority of the Federal government within their state.

Hawaii's proposed sovereignty bill comes very close to being an actual act of secession, based on native tribal rights. Hawaii was not a state at the time of Reconstruction, after the War Between the States. Texas was the only state involved in the War that did not sign the Reconstruction Doctrine and still technically retains the right to Constitutionally secede from the Union.

Tennessee passed their version of the Sovereignty Act in 2009. Its language is typical and bold. I include the Resolution below in its entirety so you can see that there is a Constitutional logic to this declaration of independence for each state from the Federal government.

> WHEREAS, the Tenth Amendment to the Constitution of the United States reads as follows: "The powers not delegated to the United States by the Constitution, nor prohibited by it to the States, are reserved to the States respectively, or to the people"; and

---

[25] http://tenthamendmentcenter.com/the-10th-amendment-movement/

WHEREAS, the Tenth Amendment defines the total scope of federal power as being that specifically granted by the Constitution of the United States and no more; and

WHEREAS, the scope of power defined by the Tenth Amendment means that the federal government was created by the states specifically to be an agent of the states; and

WHEREAS, today, in 2009, the states are demonstrably treated as agents of the federal government; and

WHEREAS, many powers assumed by the federal government and federal mandates are directly in violation of the Tenth Amendment to the Constitution of the United States; and

WHEREAS, the United States Supreme Court has ruled in New York v. United States, 112 S. Ct. 2408 (1992), that Congress may not simply commandeer the legislative and regulatory processes of the states; and

WHEREAS, a number of proposals from previous administrations and some now pending from the present administration and from Congress may further violate the Constitution of the United States; now, therefore, BE IT RESOLVED BY THE HOUSE OF REPRESENTATIVES OF THE ONE HUNDRED SIXTH GENERAL ASSEMBLY OF THE STATE OF TENNESSEE, THE SENATE CONCURRING, that we hereby affirm Tennessee's sovereignty under the Tenth Amendment to the Constitution of the United States over all powers not otherwise enumerated and granted to the federal government by the Constitution of the United States. We also demand the federal government to halt and reverse its practice of assuming powers and of imposing mandates upon the states for purposes not enumerated by the Constitution of the United States.

BE IT FURTHER RESOLVED, that a committee of conference and correspondence be appointed by the Speaker of the House and of the Senate, which shall have as its charge to communicate the preceding resolution to the legislatures of the several states, to assure them that this State continues in the same esteem of their friendship and to call for a joint working group between the states to enumerate the abuses of authority by the federal government and to seek repeal of the assumption of powers and the imposed mandates.

BE IT FURTHER RESOLVED, that a certified copy of this resolution be transmitted to the President of the United States, the President of the United States Senate, the Speaker and the Clerk of the United States House of Representatives, and to each member of Tennessee's Congressional delegation.[26]

As things stand right now it looks like Oklahoma, Washington, Hawaii, Missouri, Arizona, New Hampshire, Georgia, California, Michigan and Montana will all definitely consider sovereignty bills this year. They may be joined by Arkansas, Colorado, Idaho, Indiana, Alaska, Kansas, Alabama, Nevada, Maine and Pennsylvania where legislators have pledged to introduce similar bills.

There are now at least 40 States standing up to the federal government and demanding a return to constitutional principles is a great start, but it remains to be seen whether legislatures and governors are brave enough or angry enough to follow through. As the Obama administration and the Democratic Congress push for more expansion of federal power and spending that may help provide the motivation needed for the sovereignty

---

[26] http://www.capitol.tn.gov/Bills/106/Bill/HJR0108.pdf

movement to gain resonation and become too powerful for the Federal agencies to withstand.

The landlord is coming, and he is not happy about the illegal activities being conducted on his property. The Federal agencies are about to be evicted. The following is a list of the main areas around which the States have drawn a deep line in the sand. State Sovereignty is a shield between the agency-government and the States' properties. It effectively says, "That's far enough."

This is not an exhaustive list, but it will show you how high and wide the battle's front lines have become.

State Marijuana Laws

An honest reading of the Constitution with an original understanding of the Founders and Ratifiers makes it quite clear that the federal government has no constitutional authority to override state laws on marijuana. All three branches of the federal government, however, have interpreted (and re-interpreted) the commerce clause of the Constitution to authorize them to engage in this activity, even though there's supposedly no "legal" commerce in the plant. Although alcohol is a legal drug, and I think that is responsible for nearly all violent crime and a vast majority of traffic fatalities, I agree with Benjamin Franklin that an entire society cannot be arrested. The majority of people drink responsibly, stopping short of being out of control or dangerous to themselves or others. I merely maintain that it is not the Federal government's authority to outlaw this substance. It should be left up to the States. When their productivity drops to an unacceptably low level, and school test scores reach the level of mental retardation because everyone gets stoned every day, then they will come full circle and outlaw it again. The point is that this decision rests with the States and not with the Federal government, constitutionally speaking.

TSA

In response to increased "security" measures forced upon the people at airports around the country – naked body scanners, "enhanced pat downs," and more, legislation is being proposed to protect the right of the people to be secure in "their persons, houses, papers, and effects."

This is the second most unpopular agency that has ever been created. The IRS is the first, and I will cover that later. In June of 2011, Texas Governor Rick Perry, the nation's longest serving governor, asked the State legislature to revive a Texas bill criminalizing "intrusive" pat downs by airport security personnel. Texans were mad as hell and did not want to be searched by being physically patted down before boarding a plane. This act would have likely resulted in two things.

First, dozens of States would follow, effectively nullifying the Department of Homeland Security's authority over private airports and passengers boarding planes in those States.

Second, the Federal government would establish a "blockade" over Texas, forbidding any plane taking off from any Texas airport.

Texas backed down; however, on March 14, 2012 one of America's busiest airports, Orlando Sanford International, has announced it will opt out of using TSA workers to screen passengers, a move which threatens the highly unpopular federal agency's role in other airports across the nation.

"The president of the airport said Tuesday that he would apply again to use private operators to screen passengers, using federal standards and oversight," reports the Miami Herald.

Sanford International was prevented by the TSA from opting out back in November 2010 when the federal agency froze the ability for airports to use their own private screeners, which was a violation of State commerce laws. The Senate moved, under incredible pressure from their constituents, to require the TSA to consider applications by States to conduct the security operations without the use of TSA enforcement officers. [27]

The States have been empowered to nullify Transportation Safety Administration officers continuing to operate at State-run airports. State by State, I predict there will be a national elimination of the TSA. The argument over the quality of the safety will be made from a Federal level, but the true effect is the assertion of Federal authority to house its troops inside private businesses and on State property while forcing those States to pay for that process. This is precisely, exactly one of the original grievances of the colonies against King George that sparked the Declaration of Independence in 1776.

The Federal TSA authorities have found themselves not only outside the Constitution, but outside the favor of Americans as well. The net effect of a State loss of the right to operate airports, train stations, bus stations, and highways without the TSA will be tacit to a victory by the very terrorists that precipitated the formation of the TSA and the Department of Homeland Security. The liberty of Americans was abdicated to the Federal government by Congress in response to an Executive demand after the events of September 11, 2001.

The resistance to this act by American citizens has been building to the point of widespread open contempt after thousands of innocent passengers reported horror stories about illegal body searches and seizures of private property by TSA officers. The stories are chillingly similar to those recorded by Jews during the Nazi Third Reich. Hundreds of criminal cases involving molestation, theft, and assault have been filed against TSA officers.

National Defense Authorization Act (NDAA): Liberty Preservation Act

State by State, Legislatures independently found that the enactment into law by the United States Congress of Sections 1021 and 1022 of the

---

[27] *Major US Airport To Evict TSA Screeners* by Joseph Watson March 14, 2012 issue of InfoWars Magazine

National Defense Authorization Act of 2012, and signed into law in December of 2011, Public Law Number 112-81, is inimical to the liberty, security and well-being of those State citizens. They are declaring that the NDAA was adopted by the United States Congress in violation of the limits of Federal power in United States Constitution. As of the writing of this book, 40 States have included this declaration in State Sovereignty Acts and other actions to preserve the liberty of their citizens.

Congress shall make no law that encroaches on the following:

- Article I Section 9, Clause 2's right to seek Writ of *Habeas Corpus*;
- The First Amendment's right to petition the Government for a redress of grievances;
- The Fourth Amendment's right to be free from unreasonable searches and seizures;
- The Fifth Amendment's right to be free from charge for an infamous or capitol crime until presentment of indictment by a Grand Jury;
- The Fifth Amendment's right to be free from deprivation of life, liberty, or property, without Due Process of law;
- The Sixth Amendment's right in criminal prosecutions to enjoy a speedy trial by an impartial jury in the State and District where the crime shall have been committed;
- The Sixth Amendment's right to be informed of the nature and cause of the accusation;
- The Sixth Amendment's right to confront witnesses;
- The Sixth Amendment's right to Counsel;
- The Eighth Amendment's right to be free from excessive bail and fines, and cruel and unusual punishment;
- The Fourteenth Amendment's right to be free from deprivation of life, liberty, or property, without Due Process of law;

As of the writing of this book, it has only been about 90 days since the NDAA was signed into law, and it has not been tested in court. Certain amendments to the NDAA that were initially rejected by the Senate, but were specifically placed back into the bill by President Obama. In fact,

Mr. Obama's specific point of law allows Federal troops to arrest and detain without charges and without access to legal counsel, and to deport that individual without due process, without Habeas Corpus, and without redress.

It is unlikely that a Supreme Court test case can be formed. Victims of action taken in compliance with this law would simply disappear without due process from the population and be effectively deported from society, making it impossible for that victim's rights to be asserted. No one except those closest to the victim, or witnesses to the arrest, would have any knowledge of the Federal action. Witnesses and defenders could simply be apprehended as well, and removed for *questioning,* only to disappear as well. Unilateral targeting of Americans deemed by the President to be enemies of the State was foreseen by the founding fathers and is the reason why the Constitution was designed in the first place. Enemies of the State may be Americans exercising their right to political free speech, or to vote for an opponent, or to gather in a public place. The NDAA effectively removes the Judicial Branch from the process, in complete violation of the Constitution.

States are passing this Liberty Preservation Act to preemptively form a challenge to the NDAA, should any Federal troops be ordered to conduct its activities inside that State. The ejection of Federal troops from any State will be exactly the action taken by South Carolina beginning on April 11, 1861.

Major Robert Anderson and 87 officers and other Federal troops were holed up in the impregnable Fort Sumter, the last four months without relief or provisions. General Beauregard sent three envoys, Colonel James Chesnut, Jr., Captain Stephen D. Lee, and Lieutenant A. R. Chisolm, to offer Major Anderson a peaceful request to leave the territory with their weapons, supplies, and would even have been allowed to carry and salute the American flag on their safe journey.

Anderson thanked them for such "fair, manly, and courteous terms." Yet he stated, "It is a demand with which I regret that my sense of honor, and of my obligation to my Government, prevent my compliance." Anderson added grimly that he would be starved out in a few days—if the Confederate cannon that ringed the harbor didn't batter him to pieces first. As the envoys departed and the sound of their oars faded away across the gunmetal-gray water, Anderson knew that civil war was probably only hours away.[28]

On Friday, April 12, 1861, at 4:30 a.m., Confederate batteries opened fire, firing for 34 straight hours, on the fort. Edmund Ruffin, noted Virginian agronomist and secessionist, claimed that he fired the first shot on Fort Sumter. His story has been widely believed, but Lieutenant Henry S. Farley, commanding a battery of two mortars on James Island fired the first shot at 4:30 A.M. (Detzer 2001, pp. 269–71). No attempt was made to return the fire for more than two hours.

When the bombardment was completed, amazingly, not one single man was killed inside that fort. One Union soldier died and another was mortally wounded during the Fort's 47th shot of a 100 shot salute, allowed by the Confederacy. Afterword the salute was shortened to 50 shots. Accounts, such as in the famous diary of Mary Chesnut, describe Charleston residents along what is now known as The Battery, sitting on balconies and drinking salutes to the start of what Southerners still refer to as *the recent unpleasantness*.[29] Anderson and his men were escorted out of Charleston safely.

With this one eviction, carried out with almost zero loss of life, 13 American States declared their independence from the Federal tyranny of taxation without proper representation. President Lincoln apparently did not have the statesmanship to bring the taxation and tariff issues to a compromise between the highly-populated industrial Northern States and the sparsely populated agrarian Southern States. His answer was to declare war against the independence movement, the same decision made by King George 76 years earlier.

---

[28] History & Archaeology: *Fort Sumter: The Civil War Begins* by Fergus M. Bordewich April, 2011 issue
[29] http://en.wikipedia.org/wiki/Battle_of_Fort_Sumter

Lincoln's efforts were not met with success. The North lost every single battle and skirmish from the battle at Fort Sumter until the battle of Gettysburg ending July 3rd, 1863. During that epic battle, General Lee tried to vanquish the Union army in one massive assault. He lost. In fact, more Americans died during this three-day battle than in any conflict in history. Nearly 30 thousand were wounded.

Lincoln, although not a statesman, was a superb politician. In less than four months, he commissioned the construction of a huge memorial gravesite for the fallen soldiers of that battle. The staging of one of the greatest political victories in history was complete. While giving the greatest speech of his career, using the backdrop of nearly 8 thousand white gravestones in rows upon rows behind the Gettysburg memorial stage in the Fall afternoon of November 19th, 1863, Lincoln was successful in winning the support of Congress to fund his war of Northern Aggression.

This one event won him unswerving support from Congress and unlimited financing to order his generals as the angels of God, to sweep all living things from the Earth in their path as they marched for the capitol of the Confederacy. Driven over the edge of revenge, the Northern aristocracy threw their unquestioning support behind him. They were no longer amused with the conflict. They were driven by a vitriolic hatred of the South, coalesced by the masterful Lincoln and his timeless speech.

I include the speech below, so you can imagine sitting on a white chair in your Sunday best in a gentle Fall breeze in Pennsylvania with the military band playing patriotic music, and the stark image of immaculate headstones laid out as far as the eye can see bringing your heart up into your throat. If you are from the South, you would carefully and quietly find the nearest exit and go home to await annihilation. If you're from the North, the emotions are very similar to those we felt when President George W. Bush stood on a pile of rubble in New York City after the events of September 11, 2001. Patriotism can be a political weapon of unspeakable power, when vested with the right production quality. Listen to Lincoln's words as his forlorn figure makes this speech:

"Four score and seven years ago our fathers brought forth on this continent a new nation, conceived in liberty, and dedicated to the proposition that all men are created equal.

Now we are engaged in a great civil war, testing whether that nation, or any nation, so conceived and so dedicated, can long endure. We are met on a great battle-field of that war. We have come to dedicate a portion of that field, as a final resting place for those who here (imagine him sweeping his long right arm out to present the sea of gravestones to you) gave their lives that that nation might live. It is altogether fitting and proper that we should do this.

But, in a larger sense, we can not dedicate, we can not consecrate, we can not hallow this ground. The brave men, living and dead, who struggled here, have consecrated it, far above our poor power to add or detract. The world will little note, nor long remember what we say here, but it can never forget what they did here. It is for us the living, rather, to be dedicated here to the unfinished work which they who fought here have thus far so nobly advanced. It is rather for us to be here dedicated to the great task remaining before us—that from these honored dead we take increased devotion to that cause for which they gave the last full measure of devotion—that we here highly resolve that these dead shall not have died in vain—that this nation, under God, shall have a new birth of freedom—and that government of the people, by the people, for the people, shall not perish from the earth."[30]

In short, with 287 words he convinced the nation to finish what he had started by empowering him to use all means necessary, regardless of the Constitution, to defeat the South.

---

[30] Lincoln's Gettysburg Address (parenthesis added) November 19th, 1863.

In the year 2012, it is not just the 13 States of the South that are declaring independence from Federal rule. The stage is now set for 40 States to declare an end to Federal tyranny by removing the agency government and declaring that they, the States of America, are going to follow the Constitution as it was designed. The NDAA is the most blatant violation of the Bill of Rights ever attempted by a U.S. president. So far it has been met with almost no opposition in Washington. If the States do not act to emasculate the Act now, they will most assuredly conflict with Federal forces in their municipalities.

Health Care Freedom Act

The Health Care Freedom Act is considered in States as either a bill or a state constitutional amendment – effectively prohibiting the enactment of any new government-run healthcare programs within the State. The seizure of sole management of the health care industry has been the most widely covered disagreement between the Federal government and the States. It makes up about 15% of the gross national product. No one on either side has made a distinction between health care and health insurance. Health care has always been provided to all Americans, and even visitors to this country—legal or illegal—without charge when necessary. 85% of Americans can afford their own health care by utilizing any one of the public health clinics, private clinics, and even emergency rooms at most major hospitals. When they receive treatment, they simply pay the bill. For my family of four children and wife, I paid my own way as I went. I estimate I saved enough money to pay off two houses over the years my children were at home. I spent an average of about $750 a year in health care including all the drugs we regularly ingested like birth control, hypertension, and the occasional set of stitches. Health insurance would have cost us $9,600 a year. Over the 24 years that I had kids at home, we saved more than $205 thousand. 85% of Americans are in exactly the same shape.

While many of the State bills have language similar to true nullification legislation, many of them are promoted solely as a vehicle to drive a

Federal court battle – which is not nullification in its true sense. The Supreme Court is hearing the first test case after nearly 11 years of efforts by the Democrat party to take control of the health care industry and the massive amounts of individually mandated insurance required to pay for it.

Once known as *Hillarycare* and now popularly known as *Obamacare,* the Federal law would prohibit anyone from paying for their own health care, but would instead require every American to pay for a personal health insurance policy, and would control the type and level of care each person received by dictating to the health care industry what would and would not be allowed under the law. The Supreme Court is laughing their way through the 2,700 pages of the president's plan at the writing of this book.

The Federal government has found itself opposing 85% of American citizens. This battle between States rights and the Federal government is the largest and most well-publicized in America's history. With the most money and power over the citizenry at stake, the Federal government will not give up easily. Even if the Supreme Court decides the law is not Constitutional, which it most certainly is not, the agency-government will assert regulations to effectively force the implementation by bypassing the Legislative and Judicial Branches with an Executive Order.

Food Freedom Act

The Food Freedom Act is a direct nullification response to the "Food Safety and Modernization Act" from Washington D.C. The Federal Food, Drug, and Cosmetic Act is an 89-page law that also has authorized numerous *Guides* to be drafted with the full force of law. The FFA declares that food grown and produced in state, when sold in state are beyond the authority of Congress under its constitutional power to regulate commerce among the states. The FFA is primarily a Tenth Amendment challenge to the powers of Congress under the commerce clause, with food as the object.

The subject of Genetically Modified Organisms is the subject of the greatest anxiety. The FDA Food Safety Modernization Act (FSMA), the most sweeping reform of our food safety laws in more than 70 years, was signed into law by President Obama on January 4, 2011. It aims to ensure the U.S. food supply is safe by shifting the focus from responding to contamination to preventing it.[31]

The new law empowers *the Secretary* in a remarkable creation of Federal power over activities as common as growing a home garden.

> "GENERAL.—If the Secretary determines that food manufactured, processed, packed, received, or held by a facility registered under this section has a reasonable probability of causing serious adverse health consequences or death to humans or animals, the Secretary may by order suspend the registration of a facility—
> "(A) that created, caused, or was otherwise responsible for such reasonable probability; or
> "(B)(i) that knew of, or had reason to know of, such reasonable probability; and
> "(ii) packed, received, or held such food."[32]

Companies like Monsanto have engineered and released to the world food supply seeds containing DNA from organisms that would never have been evolved in nature. Blending jellyfish and cabbage genes into their own versions of corn, soybeans, rice, and wheat, they have been changing the food supply for many decades. Although they claim that these foods are safe, their patented strains cross-pollinate with naturally occurring varieties of these plants. Most of the product launches have been in starving third-world countries that cannot defend themselves against the Monsanto giant.

Monsanto's website describes their business as:

"The only business Monsanto Company is involved in is agriculture. This is why Monsanto invests both time and money in research to help create the best seed possible for farmers. Whether it's through breeding or

---

[31] http://www.fda.gov/food/foodsafety/fsma/default.htm
[32] PUBLIC LAW 111–353—JAN. 4, 2011 124 STAT. 3885 Section 201(b)

biotechnology, Monsanto is committed to research in various agricultural crops.

Here is a list of crops Monsanto invests in day after day.

- **Alfalfa**: Genuity® Roundup Ready® Alfalfa provides in-plant tolerance to Roundup® agricultural herbicide. Fewer weeds means it provides high-quality forage and hay.
- **Canola**: Genuity® offers the Roundup Ready® trait in both spring and winter canola. This trait is a tool for farmers to help manage weeds and increase yield potential, creating a win-win on their farm.
- **Corn**: For farmers today, it's all about getting the most yield out of every acre of corn, while using as few inputs as possible. Monsanto's corn traits help farmers do this by providing cutting-edge technology that protects the plant's yield.
- **Cotton**: Today, cotton growers are benefiting from second-generation and stacked trait technologies, which provide more levels of protection. Genuity® Bollgard II® with Roundup Ready® Flex represents Monsanto's newest wave of innovation with two second-generation traits stacked into one seed.
- **Sorghum**: Sorghum is an efficient crop in the conversion of solar energy and more drought-tolerant than other crops such as corn and soybeans. Monsanto continues to research and develop new hybrids to fit growers' needs.
- **Soybeans**: Whether it's a higher yielding soybean that provides a broad spectrum of weed control with the Roundup Ready® system or a soybean plant that helps reduce trans-fatty acids, Monsanto has a lot to offer soybean farmers.
- **Sugarbeets**: Fewer herbicide applications, increased yields and more sugar content all make Genuity Roundup Ready® sugarbeets attractive to many farmers.
- **Wheat**: Since acquiring the WestBred brand in 2009, Monsanto has initiated an intensive effort to incorporate breakthrough breeding technologies – developed and deployed with notable success in other row crops – in wheat."[33]

---

[33] http://www.monsanto.com/products/Pages/monsanto-agricultural-seeds.aspx

There are two quandaries created by this legislation. The first has become deciding who actually has to register with the agency. The second, and perhaps even more troublesome, is ruling which variety is actually the infestation; the organic version or the genetically engineered version.

The first quandary has been written into the law by creating a purview reaching into the local garden as follows:

> "(A) the sale of such food products or food directly to consumers by such establishment at a roadside stand or farmers' market where such stand or market is located other than where the food was manufactured or processed; (B) the sale and distribution of such food through a community supported agriculture program; and (C) the sale and distribution of such food at any other such direct sales platform as determined by the Secretary."[34]

Pay very close attention to the last five words, "…as determined by the Secretary." A home garden is interpreted by the Secretary to be a *community supported agricultural program* as soon as the garden grower takes a Zucchini down to the neighbor and requires registration with the Secretary and is subject to enforcement actions including destruction of the garden, fines, fees, and arrest. Once a case has been prosecuted, there will be court precedent to validate the Secretary's interpretation. Congress watches helplessly as the agency carefully selects litigation sequentially to strengthen the agency's progression of regulations and enforcement actions, which almost always lead to fees and fines. In other words, the agency gains the ability to levy taxes, plain and simple.

The second quandary has been challenged in American and Canadian courts, with some interesting results. Anthony Gucciardi is a health

---

[34] Et al Section Page 5. "Retail Food Establishment."

activist and wellness researcher writing for Natural News.

Biotech giant Monsanto has been genetically modifying the world's food supply and subsequently breeding environmental devastation for years, but leaked documents now reveal that Monsanto has also deeply infiltrated the United States government. With leaked reports revealing how U.S. diplomats are actually working for Monsanto to push their agenda along with other key government officials, Monsanto's grasp on international politics has never been clearer.

Amazingly, the information reveals that the massive corporation is also intensely involved in the passing and regulations concerning the very GM ingredients they are responsible for. In fact, the information released by WikiLeaks reveals just how much power Monsanto has thanks to key positions within the United States government and elsewhere. Not only was it exposed that the U.S. is threatening nations who oppose Monsanto with military-style trade wars, but that many U.S. diplomats actually work directly for Monsanto.

In 2007 it was requested that specific nations inside the European Union be punished for not supporting the expansion of Monsanto's GMO crops. The request for such measures to be taken was made by Craig Stapleton, the United States ambassador to France and partner to George W. Bush. Despite mounting evidence linking Monsanto's GM corn to organ damage and environmental devastation, the ambassador plainly calls for 'target retaliation' against those not supporting the GM crop. In the leaked documents, Stapleton states:

"Country team Paris recommends that we calibrate a target retaliation list that causes some pain across the EU since this is a collective responsibility, but that also focuses in part on the worst culprits. The list should be measured rather than vicious and must be sustainable over the long term, since we should not expect an early victory. Moving to retaliation will make clear that the current path has real costs to EU interests and could help strengthen European pro-biotech voices."

The undying support of key players within the U.S. towards Monsanto is undeniably made clear not only in this release, but in the legislative decisions taken by organizations such as the FDA and USDA. Legislative decisions such as allowing Monsanto's synthetic hormone Posilac (rBGH) to be injected into U.S. cows despite being banned in 27 countries. How did Monsanto pull this off?

The biotech juggernaut managed to infiltrate the FDA positions responsible for the approval of rBGH, going as far as instating the company's own Margaret Miller as Deputy Director of Human Safety and Consultative Services. After assuming this position, Miller reviewed her own report on the safety and effectiveness of rBGH.

Many US diplomats pawns of Monsanto's GM agenda

While it may be shocking to you if you are not familiar with the corrupt influence of Monsanto, the cables also show that many US diplomats are pushing GMO crops as a strategic government and commercial imperative. Interestingly enough, the U.S. focused their efforts toward advisers to the pope specifically, due to the fact that many Catholic figureheads have openly voiced their opposition to GM foods. With this kind of political influence, is it any wonder that many food staples are now predominantly GM? Nearly 93% of U.S. soybeans are heavily modified conservatively, with many other staple crops coming in at similar numbers.

U.S. diplomats have unique opportunities to spread honest and intellectual campaigns that can serve to better mankind and end suffering, however they are instead spreading the roots of Monsanto deeper and deeper into international territory. As a substitute for the betterment of mankind, these paid-off diplomats are now spreading environment desecration and health destruction.

As if there wasn't already enough information to reveal Monsanto's corruption, the biotech giant also spends enormous amount of money lobbying government each year. Monsanto spent an astonishing $2 million lobbying the federal government in the 3rd quarter of 2011 alone, according to mainstream sources. Why so much cash? The government lobbying focuses on issues like regulations for GM crops and patent reforms. This 'legal' form of persuasion is the reason government agencies like the USDA and FDA let Monsanto roam freely.

Satisfying government officials' financial vested interest is all that matters when dealing with corrupt mega-corporations like Monsanto. As long as these financial ties continue to exist, Monsanto will continue to reign over the food supply and continue to wreak devastation to the environment, ecosystem, and humankind.

With all the bad news about Monsanto and other corporations who create and promote GMOs, here's a couple of good news items from the last couple of years to relieve some doom and gloom. Hopefully, these victories against GMO companies, one by an individual farmer in Canada, the other by a large rice collective in the USA, will inspire others to hold their ground.

Normally, bully Monsanto sues small independent farmers, forcing them to pay fees for GMO plants that grew from various sources of GMO contamination, not by the farmer's choice. But the expense and mental strain of lengthy legal procedures against a wealthy corporation with soulless attorneys is too much to bear. So many settle rather than go bankrupt with Monsanto seizing the farm.

Not this time Monsanto
A feisty Canadian commercial canola farmer, Percy Schmeiser, started his fight against Monsanto's intimidation tactics in 1998. This is not a promotion of canola, but the story of a farmer who has used, saved, and developed his own seeds on his own land for over 40 years, and his David versus Goliath struggle.

After discovering his crops had been contaminated with GMO seeds from neighboring farms and passing Monsanto trucks, he was sued by Monsanto for patent infringement. Monsanto has been in the business of intimidating farmers with a similar fate by suing them for patent infringement after their fields were contaminated from GMO farms.

This intimidation and harassment has either bankrupted farmers or forced them into signing onto Monsanto's seed plan. Big bully companies use lawsuits to financially destroy small businesses even if there is no actual violation. Schmeiser and his wife, both approaching 70, decided to fight it out on principle.

Patent law says there is no violation if a patented product is not used or stolen. After some back and forth court battles and appeals over ten years, Percy won. Monsanto agreed to settle out of court by paying for cleaning up Percy's farm and not issue a gag order (customary with settlements), which enables Percy to continue touring with his message of resisting GMO and corporate intimidation. The agreement also left Monsanto liable for any recontamination of Percy's farm.

Someone big enough challenges Bayer's GM rice

Sometimes when a big guy goes after a trouble maker, the trouble maker gets it big. In April 2011, Riceland Foods won a major case against Bayer Crop Science in the Arkansas State Court System. The case involved contamination from an experimental, unapproved GM rice, Liberty Link. Its function is withstanding unlimited use of Bayer's herbicide Liberty.

The rice that Bayer contaminated with GMOs came through Riceland Foods, the nation's largest rice co-operative that collects from USA rice farmers for distribution and export. Japan simply banned all rice from America, and EU nations insisted on strict inspections before committing to any purchases. Both regions are resisting GMOs.

Riceland was awarded $11.8 million in compensatory damages and $125 million in punitive damages. The jury also decided that Bayer was responsible for any loses from GMO contamination claimed by rice farmers. Indeed, exactly a year earlier for Riceland's victory. Arkansas rice farmers had been awarded $5.9 million in compensatory damages and $42 million as punitive damages.

There are rice farmers in other states in line with suits pending on Bayer also. Monsanto must be a little concerned. They now contract farmers with a clause that makes the farmer liable for contaminating other farms. So there is some hope.

Intrastate Commerce Act

The founding fathers meant to empower Congress to regulate the buying and selling of products made by others (and sometimes land), associated finance and financial instruments, and navigation and other carriage, across State jurisdictional lines. The agency-government now has, through reams of Federal regulations written by numerous agencies, encumbered States rights to manage this, allowing banks to consolidate across State lines, creating in effect national banks with asset bases of real property and cash from numerous States' holdings.

States are attempting to reassert this original meaning of the commerce clause over wide areas of policy and effectively nullify federal laws and regulations that violate such limitations by regulating commerce and other activities that are solely intrastate. The Act states:

> "All goods grown, manufactured or made in any State and all services, performed in that State, when such goods or services are sold, maintained, or retained within that State, shall not be subject to the authority of the Congress of the United States under its constitutional power to regulate commerce among the several states..."[35]

The implications of this State legislation, if enacted with this universal core language, will be far reaching indeed. The regulations that would be shed from commerce on all levels could be the single largest stimulus to small business ever. Each State would have control of everything from finance to environmental concerns with national implications as a consideration. For instance, Atlanta may not care about its air pollution that blows away every afternoon with a gentle westerly wind.

---

[35] The Intrastate Commerce Act: paragraph (f).

The southern Tennessee Pisgah mountains have trees that are dying from acid rain fed by that pollution. Georgia environmental management must consider the damage to neighboring ecologies. This is simple and straightforward without an over-reaching, all-powerful Environmental Protection Agency making examples out of one business after another through a terrorizing process of levying enormous fines. The States can manage this between themselves through correlative legislation or through litigation by those seeking remedy without such a Federal agency being involved.

Businesses may only be able to do business inside that State for a while, but cooperating States could allow interstate commerce between them. The entire concept of import and export without duty between States is the normal modus for business. It is not logical nor conceivable that any State has the desire to isolate itself from any other State economically. A small set of laws to govern the transfer of goods from State to State is all that is needed. All property that contains a title—such as a car, trailer, mobile home, etc.—is managed on a unique State system. There is no national auto title. Each State honors the serial number and ownership of that item when the person moves to a new State.

There is no need for the Federal government to get involved, unless a State refuses to cooperate. Let's say you own a Hummer—the most polluting vehicle of modern times—and you wish to move to California. California could forbid you from registering any vehicle that does not get at least 30 miles per gallon. They could. I didn't say they would. After all, California has the third highest State tax on gasoline in the nation behind Washington and then North Carolina. All three of those States have pristine wilderness and world-class highway systems that they seek to preserve with those funds.

Still, the concept that they could have a radical environmental policy that discriminates against certain vehicle registrations is easy to understand. It doesn't take long to consider all the interested parties in litigation subsequent to such a policy. No car company likes to see their vehicle banned from a market. No citizen likes to be ordered to sell his Hummer before moving to California. This kind of activity is what allowed the camel of Federal Commerce management to enter the tent.

There isn't anything that allows the Federal government to control commerce in a State more than the regulations dominating each State's right to manage the banks inside that State. The founding fathers had long and sometimes violent arguments about this subject as well.

In its infancy, the nation was broke. It wasn't poor, and it wasn't third-world. It was broke. They needed to build, train, and pay an army and a navy in order to follow through with its plans to become independent from mother Britain. It wasn't going to be easy, especially with red uniforms on every street corner.

Hamilton made the impassioned argument that without the ability to borrow money on a national scale, the country would never become a reality, and even if it did, it couldn't survive without a national bank; a federal bank. Jefferson knew the pitfalls intimately. A federal bank would give the Federal government complete power over the States and thus over the people.

For nearly 200 years, banks were not allowed to cross ownership or monetary assets across State lines. Skillfully, banks placed advocates into federal office, and laws began to change. Usurping the Constitution through litigious engineering, bank shareholders were able to buy one bank after another until the neighborhood bank became the State bank, which then became the interstate bank, which then became the national bank, and now has become an industry of world banks. Litigious engineering is a now perfected process of designing a series of court cases that are easy to win in order to build *precedence*. Each case that is won can be strategically utilized as a foundation to win the next case, and the next and so on to achieve the goal. The Supreme Court is powerless to stop it, and new laws cannot retroactively stop it either. All the previous activities are *grandfathered* unless a very skillful law firm can get each previous case overturned. The process in either direction is expensive and risky, but it has been vastly more successful in favor of the Federal powers who wish to build more control.

Each time an interstate bank, like Wachovia or Third National Bank, is purchased by a larger bank, the asset base grows, and the power to restrict lending becomes absolute. When the nation's third largest bank merged with the nation's fifth largest bank, they became Fifth Third Bank. There are massive advantages for the shareholders, and zero benefits for the depositors.

If you go to any community, the smaller the better, you will very quickly be able to find the four most expensive buildings. Without failure, these will be the banks and churches. The bank does nothing. They produce nothing. They have no money of their own. They provide no useful service to any community. I stress the word *useful*. Even in the days of the frontier, the bank was a risky place to keep ones cash. It could get robbed or burn down. The owners of the bank could simply pack up the cash in the middle of the night and leave town. It happened.

It happened so many times that Roosevelt formed what today is known as the Federal Deposit Insurance Corporation. The FDIC was created in 1933 in response to the thousands of bank failures that occurred in the 1920s and early 1930s. The banks simply closed their doors and refused to give the depositors their money. The FDIC was formed to provide depositors confidence that the faith and credit of the United States of America—the federal government—was willing to guaranty their funds would be safe. The limit of what could be insured was $100,000 for a long time, and it was recently raised to $200,000.

On November 9, 2010, the FDIC issued a Final Rule implementing section 343 of the Dodd-Frank Wall Street Reform and Consumer Protection Act that provides for unlimited insurance coverage of noninterest-bearing transaction accounts. Beginning December 31, 2010, through December 31, 2012, all noninterest-bearing transaction accounts are fully insured, regardless of the balance of the account, at all FDIC-insured institutions. The unlimited insurance coverage is available to all depositors, including consumers, businesses, and government entities. This unlimited insurance coverage is separate from, and in addition to, the insurance coverage provided to a depositor's other deposit accounts held at an FDIC-insured institution.

A noninterest-bearing transaction account is a deposit account where interest is neither accrued nor paid; depositors are permitted to make an unlimited number of transfers and withdrawals; and the bank does **not** reserve the right to require advance notice of an intended withdrawal.
Please note that Money Market Deposit Accounts (MMDAs) and Negotiable Order of Withdrawal (NOW) accounts are **not** eligible for this unlimited insurance coverage, regardless of the interest rate, even if no interest is paid on the account.

On July 21, 2010, President Barack Obama signed the Dodd-Frank Wall Street Reform and Consumer Protection Act into law, which, in part, permanently raises the current standard maximum deposit insurance amount (SMDIA) to $250,000. The FDIC insurance coverage limit applies per depositor, per insured depository institution for each account ownership category.

Of course, there is a catch. When you open your account at the bank, which is now quite possible part of national or even global banking conglomerate, you will be given choices. You can pay a monthly fee to have the privilege of having your money in their system, or you can earn a slight amount of interest by utilizing the money market program. Who wouldn't? Would you rather pay $120 a year for the account number, or would you like to waive that cost and possibly make $100 a year on your average deposit value? That's a no-brainer, right?

Except for the risk that if the bank closes, you are not eligible for a penny of refund if you utilize the money market option. Here is the reality.

During the decade of the 1930's, it is estimated—there were many neighborhood banks that were so small they couldn't be tracked—that 9,000 banks failed. 4,000 banks failed in the year of 1933 alone. People put their money in, and could not get it out. It was gone. The banks has spent their money. On what? Farms, houses, business machinery all had value, admittedly worth less due to deflation (also called depression) but it was there, right? Wrong!

The banks had invested their depositors' money as though it was their own. It would be like if you gave your money to your older brother to hold onto for you. Each week, you handed over your paycheck as you were saving up to buy a used car. When your records showed you had enough to buy the car, you asked your brother for the money, but he had invested it at the dog track and lost it all.

Exactly the same thing happened with the banks. They used your money to gamble on currency trading and other speculative methods of expanding the money base. But wait a minute. Hold on, you say? I put $1,000 in the bank, and they pay me $1% interest. They loan the money out to a farmer who pays 5% interest. The bank makes 4% on the spread, right? That's simple enough to figure out. Not true at all.

The bank had nothing to start with. Your $1,000 was the only money in the deal, so their net worth went up by $1,000 with your deposit. It was your earning power, not the bank's that created the value. Their ability to borrow funds from the Federal Reserve just increased thanks to your money. They can borrow ten times your money at 0.5% and loan it out too at 5% interest. Now, their yield is more like 36% and not the mere 4% you were led to believe. Now you know why the bank builds those new buildings every few years. They need a way to spend all the money they're making off your money.

The amount of money involving depositors' money is about $60 trillion in the developed world. At the present time, banks are running about $100 trillion in bad gambling debts. Now you see why Jefferson was right and Hamilton was wrong.

This is precisely why the Commerce process must be repossessed by the States. The fall of the giant may be so great that the entire planet will be changed in a single day.

Constitutional Tender

The United States Constitution declares, in Article I, Section 10, "No State shall... make any Thing but gold and silver Coin a Tender in Payment of Debts." Constitutional Tender laws seek to nullify federal legal tender laws in the state by authorizing payment in gold and silver or a paper note backed 100% by gold or silver.

Why did the founding fathers specifically name gold and silver the legal tender? Alchemy. I know what you're thinking, but hear me out. Alchemy is much more than chemistry. It is a philosophy that was introduced, so the legend goes, by off-world intelligence. Yes, that is what I said. Biblical texts mention a race of off-world beings that came to Earth and taught secret combinations to men who lusted after power and wealth. We never have a shortage of such men, so the job was all too easy.

One of the easiest principles to teach was that of alchemy. History tells us that it was simply the art of changing base metals into noble metals like silver or gold. This is the embodiment of the principle, because men or historians are generally speaking, stupid. The true principle is the art of turning road gravel into gold. That is to say, make something completely worthless become legal tender for something of value.

Well the government started out with gold and silver, but the banks quickly discovered two things. First, people would not entrust them with gold on deposit. Second, there wasn't enough gold laying around to make into legal tender. A measure of gold buys exactly the same today as it did in 1850. The value of gold does not change. The value of the money is what changes on a minute by minute basis.

That brings us to the legal tender issue. When paper money was first implemented in America it had to establish support from the people and businesses who would utilize it as a federally-backed contract to pay. This was covered in great detail in Volume One of *The Ark of Millions of Years* as the Freemason leadership had the major influence over the process of crating currency for America.

I don't think there is any doubt now about the infusion of Freemason symbolism throughout the currency, the layout of Washington D.C. and the architecture of the government. Most historians agree that it provided a perception of age and wisdom that gave the people, who would be citizens of a newly born nation, and the international community confidence that America could be successful and trustworthy. It would take another chapter for me to explain the details and would also take us off the straight course I have set for this book.

The alchemy of paper currency was accepted by the world as the world standard for value for more than 200 years. Though several monetary systems were proposed for the early republic, the dollar was approved by Congress in a largely symbolic resolution on August 8, 1785. After passage of the Constitution was secured, the government turned its attention to monetary issues again in the early 1790s under the leadership of Alexander Hamilton, the secretary of the treasury at the time. Congress acted on Hamilton's recommendations in the Coinage Act of 1792, which established the dollar as the basic unit of account for the United States. The word "dollar" is derived from Low Saxon "*thaler*", an abbreviation of "*Joachimsthaler*" – (coin) from Joachimsthal– so called because it was minted from 1519 onwards using silver extracted from a mine which had opened in 1516 near Joachimstal, a town in the Ore Mountains of northwestern Bohemia.

In the early 19th century, gold rose in relation to silver, resulting in the removal from commerce of nearly all gold coins, and their subsequent melting.

The discovery of large silver deposits in the Western United States in the late 19th century created a large influx of silver, and the value of silver in the nation's coinage dropped precipitously. The argument over the value of money was hotter than ever, as silver was dropped as the second metal to back the dollar.

On one side was the United States Greenback Party that wanted to retain the bimetallic standard in order to inflate the dollar, which would allow farmers to more easily repay their debts. On the other side were Eastern banking and commercial interests, who advocated sound money and a switch to the gold standard.

This issue split the Democratic Party in 1896. It led to the famous "cross of gold" speech given by William Jennings Bryan, and may have inspired many of the themes in *The Wizard of Oz*. Despite the controversy, the status of silver was slowly diminished through a series of legislative changes from 1873 to 1900, when a gold standard was formally adopted. The gold standard survived, with several modifications, until 1971.[36]

In the famous book, *The Wizard of Oz,* by L. Frank Baum, the slippers worn by Dorothy were not ruby. She was told by the good witch of the North to click her heels together three times to return home to Kansas. The slippers in the book were silver. I wrote an analysis of the book as a political satire in 1994, as part of my undergraduate senior paper. This was Mr. Baum's symbolism for returning the nation *home* to the silver standard of money. The cowardly lion and the wizard were icons for William Jennings Bryant, the populist candidate that could never quite muster the courage to successfully run for president.

By 1971, there were no metals backing the American dollar. The alchemy of turning of high-quality linen paper into gold had finally been completed. The unfolding of the ancient plan is happening exactly as we predicted it would in Volume Two of *The Ark of Millions of Years* by converting dollars into ones a zeroes by computers owned by the Federal Reserve.

Money is created with a simple keystroke for electronic transfer of numbers between accounts. Value, however, is not fabricated so easily. When you look at the numbers in your account, you see the balance left after all the debits are subtracted from the credits. In reality, there is no money in your account. There is only a measure of the value produced through your work or your investment.

The conversion of that work-value you created with your skill in Mississippi is transferred across State lines to an e-bay shop in New York, who then drop ships a new pair of headphones to your address. The numbers are moved around, and commerce is completed. That is as long

---

[36] http://en.wikipedia.org/wiki/History_of_the_United_States_dollar

as the numerical value in your PayPal account is higher that the value of the headphones you are purchasing. That sounds simple enough, doesn't it?

You never stop to think about the actual value of the numbers in the account. Your hours of work have been effectively exchanged for headphones. Nice, neat, and clean.

But what happens if you don't have a high enough value in your account to buy the headphones? Exactly. You wait until you do have enough. Not if you are the Federal government. You simply call up the Federal Reserve and order them to add some numbers to the government's account, and off you go. This creates a deficit.

Deficit spending is the amount by which a government, private company, or individual's spending exceeds income over a particular period of time, also called simply "deficit", or "budget deficit", the opposite of budget surplus. Like all universes, the number that the Federal Reserve can create for anyone is not infinite. There is an absolutely smallest form of measurement, called resolution. If we have a limited resolution, we have a limited universe. There is no possible doubt about it.

Lack of sound money has done more to coalesce the subterfuge of alchemy into the alienated nation of America than anything else. The Federal government has exhausted all the numbers the Federal Reserve can alchemically create. The end of the currency universe has been reached. There is nothing more than a promise to pay, half a century in the future.

The return of Constitutional Tender to the American dollar is going to be as painful as any addict quitting their habit. The value of the dollar is so low that numerous foreign countries have called for another currency to become the world standard. The Federal Reserve has done exactly what it set out to do when it was created by the Federal government in 1907. It was created on December 23, 1913 with the enactment of the Federal

Reserve Act, largely in response to a series of financial panics, particularly a severe panic in 1907.[37]

According to the Board of Governors, the Federal Reserve is independent within government in that "its monetary policy decisions do not have to be approved by the President or anyone else in the executive or legislative branches of government." Its authority is derived from statutes enacted by the U.S. Congress and the System is subject to congressional oversight. The members of the Board of Governors, including its chairman and vice-chairman, are chosen by the President and confirmed by the Senate.

The primary motivation for creating the Federal Reserve System was to address banking panics. Other purposes are stated in the Federal Reserve Act, such as "to furnish an elastic currency, to afford means of rediscounting commercial paper, to establish a more effective supervision of banking in the United States, and for other purposes". Before the founding of the Federal Reserve, the United States underwent several financial crises. A particularly severe crisis in 1907 led Congress to enact the Federal Reserve Act in 1913. Today the elastic Federal Reserve System has been stretched far past the limit. Deficit spending by America and Europe has far exceeded the alchemical limit of the program. It may be only moments before the elastic system snaps.

Firearms Freedom Act
Originally introduced and passed in Montana, the FFA declares that any firearms made and retained in-state are beyond the authority of Congress under its constitutional power to regulate commerce among the states. The FFA is primarily a Tenth Amendment challenge to the powers of Congress under the commerce clause, with firearms as the object.

The founding fathers knew at the end of the day, that the one thing that would keep a government from oppressing its citizens is the right of the citizenry to own firearms. There are more firearms in America than there

---

[37] Born of a panic: Forming the Federal Reserve System". The Federal Reserve Bank of Minneapolis. August 1988. www.minneapolisfed.org/pubs/region/88-08/reg888a.cfm.

are people in the country. No government could possibly hope to oppress a nation so armed.

There are several versions of the text of the Second Amendment, each with slight capitalization and punctuation differences, found in the official documents surrounding the adoption of the Bill of Rights. One version was passed by the Congress, while another is found in the copies distributed to the States and then ratified by them.

As passed by the Congress:
> A well regulated Militia, being necessary to the security of
> a free State, the right of the people to keep and bear Arms,
> shall not be infringed.
> As ratified by the States and authenticated by Thomas
> Jefferson, Secretary of State:
> A well regulated militia being necessary to the security of
> a free state, the right of the people to keep and bear arms
> shall not be infringed.

The original hand-written copy of the Bill of Rights, approved by the House and Senate, was prepared by scribe William Lambert and resides in the National Archives.

One can only speculate as to why various agencies of the government are working to eliminate this most explicit right to bear arms. I try not to proliferate conspiracy theories. There is, however, no denying that the courts are being used in the classic manner of litigious legislation by stacking one court victory over another to unarm America. One thing most people miss is the intentional and meticulous manner in which registrations for firearms purchases have changed.

Under the Gun Control Act of 1968, the Bureau of Alcohol, Tobacco and Firearms, now the Bureau of Alcohol, Tobacco, Firearms, and Explosives (BATFE) was given wide latitude on the enforcement of regulations pertaining to Federal Firearms License (FFL) holders. Allegations of abuse by ATF inspectors soon arose from the National Rifle Association (NRA) and certain targeted Federal firearms licensees.

In the *Report of the Subcommittee on the Constitution of the Committee on the Judiciary, United States Senate, 97th Congress, Second Session* (February 1982), a bipartisan subcommittee (consisting of 3 Republicans and 2 Democrats) of the United States Senate investigated the Second Amendment and reported its findings. The report stated:

The conclusion is thus inescapable that the history, concept, and wording of the second amendment to the Constitution of the United States, as well as its interpretation by every major commentator and court in the first half century after its ratification, indicates that what is protected is an individual right of a private citizen to own and carry firearms in a peaceful manner.[38] It concluded that seventy-five percent of Bureau of Alcohol, Tobacco, Firearms and Explosives prosecutions were "constitutionally improper", especially on Second Amendment issues.[39]

The Firearm Owners Protection Act of 1986 addressed the abuses noted in the 1982 Senate Judiciary Subcommittee report. Among the reforms intended to loosen restrictions on gun ownership were the reopening of interstate sales of long guns on a limited basis, legalization of ammunition shipments through the U.S. Postal Service (a partial repeal of the Gun Control Act), removal of the requirement for record keeping on sales of non-armor-piercing ammunition, and federal protection of transportation of firearms through states where possession of those firearms would otherwise be illegal. However, the act also contained a provision that banned the sale of machine guns manufactured after the date of enactment to civilians, restricting sales of these weapons to the military and law enforcement. Thus, in the ensuing years, the limited supply of these arms available to civilians has caused an enormous increase in their price, with most costing in excess of $10,000. Regarding these fully automatic firearms owned by private citizens in the United States, political scientist Earl Kruschke said "approximately 175,000 automatic firearms have been licensed by the Bureau of Alcohol, Tobacco, and Firearms (the federal agency responsible for administration of the law) and evidence suggests

---

[38] Right to Keep and Bear Arms, U.S. Senate. 2001 Paladin Press. ISBN 1581602545.
[39] "Gun Law News: Firearm Owners Protection Act of 1986".

that none of these weapons has ever been used to commit a violent crime."[40]

The gun rights movement lobbied Congress to pass the FOPA to prevent the abuse of regulatory power — in particular, to address claims that the ATF was repeatedly inspecting FFL holders for the apparent purpose of harassment intended to drive the FFL holders out of business (as the FFL holders would constantly be having to tend to ATF inspections instead of to customers).

The Act mandated that ATF compliance inspections can be done only once per year. An exception to the "once per year" rule exists if multiple record-keeping violations are recorded in an inspection, in which case the ATF may do a follow-up inspection. The main reason for a follow-up inspection would be if guns could not be accounted for.

The Bureau of Alcohol, Tobacco, and Firearms—yes, they are one of the most powerful and nefarious divisions of the agency-government—has used the courts to pass a regulation outlawing *armor-piercing* slugs in an effort to protect government agents who may conflict with citizens acting in a criminal manner.

18 U.S.C. Section 922(a)(7) states that it shall be unlawful "for any person to manufacture or import armor piercing ammunition. Except that this paragraph shall not apply to-(A) the manufacture or importation of such ammunition for the use of the United States or any department or agency thereof or State or any department agency, or political subdivision thereof...Further, Section 922(a)(8) specifies that it shall be unlawful "for any manufacturer or importer to sell or deliver armor piercing ammunition, except that this paragraph shall not apply to (A) the manufacture or importation of such ammunition for the use of the United States or any department or agency thereof or State or any department agency, or political subdivision thereof."

---

[40] Kruschke, Earl R. (1995). *Gun control: a reference handbook*. Santa Barbara, Calif: ABC-CLIO. pp. 85. ISBN 0-87436-695-X.

Clearly, this is a regulation that allows agencies to buy and utilize armor piercing ammunition, while forbidding the citizen to do the same. Now, to demonstrate the incrementalism that is utilized to build the regulations, notice that the regulation applied only to the use of *armor piercing ammunition* in handguns. Allegedly, these are the weapons that are most likely to be utilized in the commission of a crime.

As defined in 18 U.S.C. Section 921(a)(17)(B), the term "armor piercing ammunition" means--...(i) a projectile or projectile core which may be used in a handgun and which is constructed entirely (excluding the presence of traces of other substances) from one or a combination of tungsten alloys, steel, iron, brass, bronze, beryllium copper, or depleted uranium; or (ii) a full jacketed projectile larger than .22 caliber designated and intended for use in a handgun and whose jacket has a weight of more than 25 percent of the total weight of the projectile.

These regulations were quoted by the BATF in a letter dated June 30, 2011 pursuant to a raid on the Elite Ammunition company. They also seized all sales records and registration documents so that the buyers and shippers of the ammunition could be prosecuted as well.

Pay close attention to the following logical steps taken by the raid and the subsequent convictions of these felonies. The regulation is passed as a forethought to protect agents of the governments from conflicting with persons armed with handguns using ammunition that, by nature if its components, pierce car doors, personnel shields and helmets, and personal armored vests. The raid takes place on a perfect example of a violator. The case proceeds to victory in court. The victory is used to improve the regulation to include other weapons, namely rifles. Any bullet used in a handgun can be used in a rifle.

The BATF has effectively banned a class of ammunition, while not infringing upon the right of the citizen from owning the firearm. Step by step, the components that make ammunition will be outlawed.

A steady watch by officials for events that the agencies may utilize in a litigious legislative process to disarm Americans exists. In the Fall of

2011, a terribly botched operation mastered by the Department of Justice to trace weapons used by drug cartels in Mexico was revealed to the public when a U.S. agent was murdered by one of the very weapons the BATF *seeded* into Mexico.

In a complete lack of technological forethought, the BATF distributed thousands upon thousands of high-quality firearms to networks that would proliferate those weapons to the soldiers of the drug cartels in Mexico. No RF ID chips were placed in the guns to allow them to be tracked remotely. No self-destruct features were incorporated into the weapons to render them useless with a remote signal. No marking dye, such as that utilized by banks during a robbery, or other tracing methods were employed. The weapons were top quality, semi-automatic—easily made fully automatic with a few drop-in modifications to the sear release mechanisms—that took only a few days to see action. More than 30 thousand people were killed in Mexico as a result, and the weapons were predictably turned on the very people that proliferated them in the first place.

The agency-government feeds weapons to rebels and criminals all over the world with exactly the same results. Turn on the news any night you wish, and you will see RPG's, AK-47's, and even shoulder-fired rockets being used by common people wearing sneakers and jogging suits against helicopters and armored vehicles. The news super-model reads the script that tells you civilians are being killed in the streets, but you know our military-police would be doing the same exact thing if they were being fired upon from the streets below with effective weapons. Nobody remembers who started the violence. Laws will be enforced, no matter what coerced the violation. We think it is reprehensible when aircraft growl bullets at civilians ducking and hiding behind corner markets or mosques, but we don't blink an eye when the Department of Justice orders an entire innocent community, including women and children, to be burned to death on live television in Waco, Texas.

Crimes are committed by violating laws which prompts new regulations, which are then used to disarm the very citizens the founding fathers designed to empower with self-defense. What you see in other countries on the streets of attempted liberty all over the world is an archetype for what was foreseen by the founding fathers.

Operating on the claim of complete ignorance of the operation, called *Fast and Furious*, the Department of Justice refused to take any responsibility or prosecute anyone in the agency-government for illegal trafficking in weapons and ammunition. Slowly, the press is losing interest in the story. It no longer sells newspapers. The Attorney General, William Holder, refuses to resign or take responsibility for his department's leadership role in the deaths by the very guns his office financed and distributed. Mexico responded in the only way it could. Mexican officials yelled and stomped their feet. After all, what can they do against the US Department of Justice? Apparently, even less that we can.

Hispanic Americans who held public office in Congress reacted as well. The following is the entire text of the Joint House-Senate Resolution SRJ10 so you can see what foot stomping really sounds like.

BILL NUMBER: SJR 10
INTRODUCED BILL TEXT INTRODUCED BY   Senator De León

(Coauthors: Senators Hancock, Hernandez, Padilla, and Vargas)
(Coauthors: Assembly Members Alejo, Allen, Bonilla, Bradford, Cedillo, Davis, Eng, Roger Hernández, Hueso, Lara, Mendoza, Perea, V. Manuel Pérez, Solorio, and Torres)

JULY 5, 2011
Relative to firearms trafficking.
LEGISLATIVE COUNSEL'S DIGEST
SJR 10, as introduced, De León. Firearms trafficking.
This measure would urge the President and the Congress of the United States to pursue a comprehensive approach to stem the trafficking of illicit United States firearms into Mexico, that includes, among other things, the redirection of federal Bureau of Alcohol, Tobacco, Firearms and Explosives (ATF), United States
Immigration and Customs Enforcement, and United States Customs and Border Protection resources towards this effort, reenactment of a strong

114

federal assault weapons ban, adoption of the ATF's proposed rule to require the reporting of rifle, including assault rifle, purchases in southwestern border states, and stronger federal
authority to crack down on corrupt gun dealers.

"WHEREAS, The rise of firearms trafficking from the United States into Mexico has fueled the terrorism of both United States and Mexican citizens by Mexican drug trafficking organizations (DTOs), that has devastated thousands of families who have lost loved ones to violence on both sides of the border; and

WHEREAS, Since the start of Mexican President Felipe Calderon's administration in December 2006, the Mexican law enforcement agencies have confiscated 102,600 handguns and rifles as of March 10, 2011, and Mexican security forces have seized 11,849 grenades and 10.6 million rounds of ammunition; and

WHEREAS, Violence along the United States-Mexico border has escalated dramatically during this same timeframe as President Calderon has aggressively fought the growing power of Mexican DTOs and over 23,000 people have been killed as a result of drug cartel violence in Mexico; and

WHEREAS, In a report by the United States Government Accountability Office (GAO), United States officials note that violence associated with Mexican DTOs poses a serious challenge for United States law enforcement and particularly given the increased level of criminal activity in the southwestern United States,
violence threatens the safety of citizens on both sides of the border; and

WHEREAS, In May 2010, the Mexican government stated that of the 75,000 illegal firearms it seized in the last three years, about 80 percent--60,000 firearms--came from the United States; and

WHEREAS, Estimates of guns flowing into Mexico from the United States are as high as 2,000 guns every day, a staggering statistic given that Mexico has only approximately 6,000 legally registered guns; and

WHEREAS, The United States Bureau of Alcohol, Tobacco, Firearms and Explosives (ATF), as of May 2010, has processed 69,808 firearm trace requests from Mexico and it appears that a majority of these firearms have a nexus to the United States; and

WHEREAS, There are more than 6,600 licensed United States gun dealers operating along the United States-Mexico border and according to several ATF officials, individuals or groups engage in straw purchasing on a regular basis as part of a scheme to traffic United States firearms into Mexico; and

WHEREAS, The ATF reports that 87 percent of firearms seized by Mexican authorities and traced over the last five years originated in the United States, that approximately 68 percent of these illegal firearms were manufactured in the United States, and approximately 19 percent were manufactured in other countries and then imported into the United States before being trafficked into Mexico; and

WHEREAS, ATF officials state that the most common method of transporting firearms illegally across the United States-Mexico border is by vehicle using United States highways, and that an opportune time to catch firearm smugglers is following a United States gun show in Arizona or Texas; and

WHEREAS, Operation Armas Cruzadas was established by the United States Immigration and Customs Enforcement (ICE) in 2008, and the United States Department of Homeland Security states that this effort has resulted in the seizure of 3,877 weapons and 396,424 rounds of ammunition; and

WHEREAS, Project Gunrunner was initiated by the ATF, with the objective of tracing firearms recovered from crimes in Mexico, and although the tactics utilized by this program are currently under scrutiny, by the end of the 2009 fiscal year, the ATF referred 497 cases to the United States

Department of Justice to pursue the prosecution of firearms trafficking violations to Mexico; and

WHEREAS, Since 2006, 14 United States Custom and Border Patrol (CBP) Agents have been killed in Mexico, most recently Agent Brian Terry, who was killed on December 15, 2010, by being shot with an AK-47; and

WHEREAS, In February 2011, ICE Special Agent Jaime Zapata was shot and killed and another federal agent was wounded in an ambush by Mexican drug gang members at a fake military checkpoint on a Mexican highway north of Mexico City; and

WHEREAS, DTOs have escalated the use of firearms to attack and intimidate high level Mexican law enforcement figures, including directors of federal agencies, politicians, journalists, businesses, and the general public; and

WHEREAS, Mexican government officials report that since December 2006, a total of 915 municipal police, 698 state police, and 463 federal agents have been killed by Mexican Organized Crime Groups (OCGs), and between 1999 and 2009, 32 news reporters or editors were killed and an additional nine disappeared; and

WHEREAS, On June 28, 2010, a leading Mexican gubernatorial candidate, Rodolfo Torre Cantu, was killed by gunfire in Tamaulipas, just days before the July 4, 2010, elections, and in late 2008, Armando Rodriguez, a crime reporter for El Diario de Juárez, was shot in the head by a 9mm as he drove his daughter to school; and

WHEREAS, In June 2008, Edgar Millan Gomez, acting director of the federal preventive police was assassinated in his own home by a man wielding two 9mm pistols one week after holding a press conference in Cuiliacán to announce the arrests of 12 hit men working for the Sinaloa Cartel and that same day, Roberto Velasco, one of the directors of the federal organized crime unit, was shot and killed in Mexico City, and the next day Jose Aristeo, chief of staff for the federal preventive police, was shot and killed in the same city; and

WHEREAS, United States citizens have also been terrorized by the violence associated with United States firearms trafficking and Mexican DTOs. For example, in May 2010, a Phoenix businessman leading a hunting expedition in Sonora, Mexico was found shot dead by an AK-47, in February 2010, United States and Mexican citizens waiting to cross into Mexico from Nogales, Arizona were trapped in a firefight that erupted in the nearby plaza, in the spring of 2008 American tourists returning through the Lukeville port of entry were
trapped by gunfire while waiting in line, and a woman from Nogales, Arizona was shot and killed by AK-47 gunfire at a fake military checkpoint on a Mexican interstate in Sonora; and

WHEREAS, The ATF proposed a new federal rule in 2010 that would require all United States gun stores in southwest border states to submit a report to ATF when an individual purchases two or more rifles, including assault rifles, within five business days, and ATF' s proposed rule has not yet been adopted; and

WHEREAS, Following the expiration of the federal Assault Weapon Ban in 2004, it has become easier to purchase high-powered assault weapons and the United States Department of Justice, Office of the
Inspector General has reported that 48 percent of crime guns recovered and traced in Mexico in 2009 were long guns, up from 20 percent in 2004 and recent data also shows a surge in seizures of assault rifles and .50 caliber guns. According to the ATF, the drug cartels tend to favor military-style assault weapons such as AK-47s,
AR-15s, and FN 5.7mm caliber pistols, known in Mexico as "cop killers" because they can pierce body armor; and

WHEREAS, The United States is now experiencing an era in which the number of illegal border crossings have decreased over the last decade yet drug-related violence and the trafficking of United States firearms into Mexico has skyrocketed;

NOW, THERFORE, BE IT RESOLVED by the Senate and the Assembly of the State of California, jointly, That the Legislature urges the President and the Congress of the United States to pursue a comprehensive approach to stem the trafficking of illicit United States firearms into Mexico, that includes the redirection of United States Alcohol, Tobacco, Firearms, and Explosives (ATF), Immigration and Customs Enforcement, and Customs and Border Protection resources towards this effort, reenactment of a strong federal assault weapons ban, along with a ban on high-capacity ammunition magazines, adoption of the ATF's proposed rule to require the reporting of rifle, including assault rifle, purchases in southwestern border states, stronger federal authority to crack down on corrupt gun dealers, extending Brady criminal background checks to all gun sales, including all sales at gun shows to prevent firearms trafficking, and the maintenance of firearm purchase records to help law enforcement track down armed criminals and solve gun crimes; and be it further Resolved, That the Secretary of the Senate transmit copies of this resolution to the President and Vice President of the United States, to the Speaker of the House of Representatives, to the Majority leader of the Senate, to each Senator and Representative from California in the Congress of the United States, and to the author for appropriate distribution."

As of the writing of this book, the agency-government has shown no compunction to prosecute anyone connected with Operation Fast and Furious. No one has been arrested. No one has resigned.

REAL ID Act
The **REAL ID Act of 2005**, Pub.L. 109-13, 119 Stat. 302, enacted May 11, 2005, was an Act of Congress that modified U.S. federal law pertaining to security, authentication, and issuance procedures standards for the state driver's licenses and identification (ID) cards, as well as various immigration issues pertaining to terrorism.

The law set forth certain requirements for state driver's licenses and ID cards to be accepted by the federal government for "official purposes", as defined by the Secretary of Homeland Security. The Secretary of Homeland Security has currently defined "official purposes" as presenting state driver's licenses and identification cards for boarding commercially operated airline flights and entering federal buildings and nuclear power plants.

As of April 2, 2008, all 50 States have either applied for extensions of the original May 11, 2008 compliance deadline or received unsolicited extensions.[41]

As of October 2009, 25 states have approved either resolutions or binding legislation not to participate in the program, and with President Obama's selection of Janet Napolitano (a prominent critic of the program) to head the Department of Homeland Security, the future of the law remains uncertain, and bills have been introduced into Congress to amend or repeal it.

The most recent of these, dubbed PASS ID, would eliminate many of the more burdensome technological requirements but still require states to meet federal standards in order to have their ID cards accepted by federal agencies. **PASS ID** is a proposed U.S. law intended to replace REAL ID. Like REAL ID, it implements federal standards for state identification documents. Currently, states are not obligated to follow the standards, but if PASS ID takes full effect, federal agencies will only accept identification from states that materially comply with the law. Citizens from non-compliant states would need to provide federally issued documents such as a social security card or U.S. passport in order to enter federally-owned buildings.

PASS ID would eliminate REAL ID requirements that are considered excessive, such as the obligation to verify birth certificates with the issuing department, and shared national databases. However, critics charge PASS ID will still require the storage of digital records of documents proving

---

[41] "States get real ID Extensions," USA TODAY 4-2-2008 by Mimi Hall

citizenship, such as birth certificates. It may also permit technology like RFID to be incorporated into drivers' licenses.[42]

There are two main things to consider here. First, the effort by the States to resist ID laws is not because they think unidentified people should be walking around their territory. The effort is to preserve the State's right to manage this, and to establish that this is not under the purview of the Federal government.

Second, a methodology of protecting the integrity of the election system inside each State is paramount. Federal regulations that are being resisted include language that only requires ID when conducting Federal business or boarding an airplane. There is no protection against voter fraud, a widely used tactic to manipulate elections. It is a known fact that dead people and pets vote in elections.

In a result of recent investigative reporting—wow there are real reporters out there—it was discovered that rampant voter fraud was utilized to get Barack Obama onto the Indiana ballot in 2008. Without the fraudulent signatures on the petition, Mr. Obama would not have been included in the Indiana primary election where he ran against Hillary Clinton. In each congressional district in Indiana, you need 500 signatures - Obama qualified with 534. It is has been proven after a name-by-name investigation that 150 of them were forged by members of the Obama 2008 campaign.[43]

Rep. Todd Rokita, R-IN, a former Indiana Secretary of State, told Fox News the next step: "What we have to do next is to involve the U.S. Attorney General, Eric Holder." However, Rokita said Holder has not responded to a letter he wrote requesting assistance. "He's putting people above the law," the congressman said. "He's putting his party, his boss, and his ideology above equal application of the law."

---

[42] Chad Vander Veen (Aug 14, 2009). "Is PASS ID Better Than REAL ID? (Analysis)". Government Technology Magazine/e.Republic, Inc..
[43] "Obama Election Fraud Investigation Underway in Indiana" MRCTV 12-14-2011 by Joe Schoffstall

St. Joseph County Prosecuting Attorney Mike Dvorak is investigating the fraud, but the U.S. Attorney for the Northern District of Indiana, David A. Capp, has refused. "The U.S. attorney does not investigate allegations of fraud in the submission of petitions by political parties for the placement of the names of candidates on the ballot for federal primary elections," his office wrote in an October statement.[44]

The issue boils down to the States being able to manage the identification of it citizens to protect the integrity of commerce and official business inside that State. States are being mandated to implement Federal identification processes without funding, while being completely neglected by the agency-government to prosecute identity fraud in Federal elections. Now you see why the States are drawing a unified and powerful line of solidarity in the sand by refusing to comply with Federal ID laws.

Defend the Guard

Under the Constitution, the militia (now called the National Guard) may only be called into duty by the federal government in three specific situations. According to Article I, Section 8; Clause 15, the Congress is given the power to pass laws for "calling forth the Militia to execute the Laws of the Union, suppress Insurrections and repel Invasions." The militia was intended by the founding fathers to function as a defense force and nothing more. Deployments outside the country were not considered, and neither were internal deployments in pursuance of powers that were not delegated to the federal government.

Congress has passed numerous laws in the past 100 years giving the federal government additional authority not mentioned in the Constitution. But, without amendment, altering the enumerated powers by legislative fiat is, in and of itself, unconstitutional. Campaigns in states around the country are working to reassert the authority of governors over guard troops.

---

[44] "Indiana Lawmaker: Holder Absent on Primary Petition Fraud Case" ELECTIONS section of FoxNews.com 12-18-2011 by Eric Shawn

State Rep. Aaron Libby has submitted a bill that would require Maine's governor to withhold or withdraw approval of the transfer of the Maine National Guard to federal control unless Congress declares war. The measure has broad bipartisan support and has been referred to the Veterans and Legal Affairs Committee for its consideration. Rep. Libby's bill, LD 1305, would direct Maine's governor to withhold transfer of the Maine Guard to federal control unless at least one of three constitutional provisions applied. The first is a military invasion of the United States; the second would involve an insurrection.

The third condition involves "a calling forth of the National Guard by the United States Congress, in a manner authorized by the United States Constitution, to execute the laws of the United States, so long as those laws were made in accordance with the powers delegated to the federal government in the Constitution."

The legislation requires a review by Maine's governor of every federal order that places the Maine Guard on federal duty, "including any order that is in effect on the effective date of this section," to determine whether the order complies with the Constitution. If the governor determines that the order does not meet constitutional muster, "the governor shall take all appropriate action to prevent the Maine Guard from being placed or kept on federal active duty."

It sounds great, but on May 13, 2011, the following action was taken by the Speaker of the House.

> Speaker laid before the House Subsequently, The
> House **RECEDED** and **CONCURRED** to **ACCEPTAN**
> **CE** of the Majority **Ought Not to Pass** Report.
> **ROLL CALL NO. 74**
> (Yeas 128 - Nays 13 - Absent 9 - Excused 0) (Vacancy 1)
> ORDERED SENT FORTHWITH.
> Placed in the Legislative Files. (**DEAD**)

As of the writing of this book, the President has not been limited in his application of the State Guards to Federal and foreign deployments as though the individuals had been drafted into active duty. This is a classic example of the *camel's nose* in your man cave. A new twist, I know, but the result is that citizens seek the financial benefit of serving part time in the National Guard. They are wooed by a clever marketing plan depicting disaster relief and emergency labor assistance using various skills like medical, logistics, and the good old strong back and lots of manpower. They signed up to help America when local authorities were not enough.

Not one single citizen signed up as a weekend warrior with the dream of being deployed four times in a foreign war zone and coming home with less body than they left with. People who want to break things and kill people enlist in the Federal military.

The confiscation of the State's guard personnel, including women, by the President is a violation of the original design of the National Guard. The National Guard, the oldest component of the Armed Forces of the United States and one of the nation's longest-enduring institutions, celebrated its 375th birthday on December 13, 2011. The National Guard traces its history back to the earliest English colonies in North America. Responsible for their own defense, the colonists drew on English military tradition and organized their able-bodied male citizens into militias.

The colonial militias protected their fellow citizens from Indian attack, foreign invaders, and later helped to win the Revolutionary War. Following independence, the authors of the Constitution empowered Congress to "provide for organizing, arming, and disciplining the militia." However, recognizing the militia's state role, the Founding Fathers reserved the appointment of officers and training of the militia to the states. Nothing in the charter or design represented that the President could, without Congress and without a declaration of war, order the members of the state militias to international aggression.

Since that time, the National Guard has seen the nature of its Federal mission change, with more frequent call ups in response to crises in Haiti, Bosnia, Kosovo, and the skies over Iraq. Today, tens of thousands of Guardmembers are serving in harm's way in Iraq and Afghanistan, as the National Guard continues its historic dual mission, providing to the states units trained and equipped to protect life and property, while providing to the nation units trained, equipped and ready to defend the United States and its interests, all over the globe.[45]

The citizens of the States have decided with this Defend the Guard Act that it is time for Guardmembers to come home. The phrase, "...and its interests, all over the globe," is imperialist and expands the mission of the state militia beyond the original design. It is nothing more than a bulk involuntary draft. The blood of thousands of citizens is on the hands of the Presidents who have ordered them into global aggression.

The States maintain that if the President wants a killing force to send to other countries, he needs to hire and train his own army and to leave the State militias to their domestic protection and relief. After all, who will come to the defense of the State when it is the Federal government that becomes the enemy?

Sheriffs First Legislation

A "Sheriffs First" bill would make it a state crime for any federal agent to make an arrest, search, or seizure within the state without first getting the advanced, written permission of the elected county sheriff of the county in which the event is to take place.

Imagine Andy in Mayberry sitting down for peach cobbler with aunt Bee only to discover that Floyd had been arrested for not keeping his combs in the proper solution prior to cutting Goober's hair. Surprise, surprise, surprise.

The intent of this legislation is to involve local law enforcement in the process of a search, seizure, or arrest. Of course, the National Defense Authorization Act, modified and signed into law by Mr. Obama, allows the Federal Army to take Floyd without so much as a Miranda Right being read by Barney or anyone else.

---

[45] http://www.ng.mil/About/default.aspx

The village, town, and city we once called a sovereign home is constantly searched through electronic means. Persons and property are regularly seized without due process. Arrests without *habeas corpus*—meaning produce the body—and without that call to a lawyer or appointment of a public defender are now legal and operational.

The Sheriff First Act exists, because States feel that Andy should be first to approve Floyd's arrest. Without this local veil of protection, dispassionate and uninformed Federal mistakes will be made that end innocent life. It is a harbinger of the day when local law enforcement will be on the wrong end of the Federal gun. Barney will need more than one bullet.

Cap and Trade/EPA

Cap and Trade and EPA regulations and acts are often claimed to be authorized under the Commerce Clause of the Constitution. At best, this is a highly dubious claim. This interstate regulation of "commerce" did not include agriculture, manufacturing, mining, or land use. Nor did it include activities that merely "substantially affected" commerce. The Environmental Protection Agency has been regularly excoriated before Congressional committees for litigious legislation. Their regulations are facilitated by shock and awe lawsuits against business and property owners in an engineered sequence as carefully as laying bricks for a wall; a wall to secure the border.

Many efforts have been mounted by powerful members of Congress to establish a new currency. As of the writing of this book, we have seen the dollar's alchemical instability and unreliability spawn the creation of new currencies. For a few years it was baby formula. Yes, that's what I said. Organized crime, well beyond the mere classic mafia, targeted the commodity as highly marketable, untraceable, and more reliable than cash at holding its value. Recently, female hygienic products have been added to the list of larcenous trade items. Congress is not too slow to pick up on the modus operandi.

The one thing that States share is air. The discovery of this remarkable and nearly imaginary commodity offered an irresistible opportunity to

Congress. The American Clean Energy and Security Act of 2009 (ACES) was an energy bill in the 111th United States Congress (H.R. 2454) that would have established a variant of an emissions trading plan similar to the European Union Emission Trading Scheme. The bill was approved by the House of Representatives on June 26, 2009 by a vote of 219-212, but died in the Senate.

This vote was the "first time either house of Congress had approved a bill meant to curb the heat-trapping gases scientists have linked to climate change." [46]

The bill was also known as the Waxman-Markey Bill, after its authors, Representatives Henry   A.   Waxman of   California and Edward   J. Markey of Massachusetts, both Democrats. Waxman is the chairman of the Energy and Commerce Committee, and Markey is the chairman of that committee's Energy and Power Subcommittee.

Internationally, the House's passage of the ACES bill "established a marker for the United States when international negotiations on a new climate change treaty begin later this year." The committee was formed in record time and the drafting and passage of the Bill was faster than anyone could even read the voluminous and sweeping Federal authorization to seize the air for their own. Hearings on the draft of the legislation took place the week of April 20, 2009 and the bill was passed by the House on June 26, 2009.

Now, I surmise that you are not familiar with this new commodity. You may have heard the term thrown around. But you probably have no idea how much money we are talking about. This makes baby formula and female hygiene products nothing compared to the biggest alchemical scam of all time. I know. You need the facts to back up my claim. Well, have I ever let you down?

The bill proposes a cap and trade system, under which the government sets a limit (cap) on the total amount of greenhouse gases that can be emitted

---

[46] Broder, John (2009-06-26). "House Passes Bill to Address Threat of Climate Change". New York Times. Retrieved 2009-06-27.

nationally. Companies then buy or sell permits to emit these gases, primarily carbon dioxide CO_2. The cap is reduced over time to reduce total carbon emissions. The legislation would set a cap on total emissions over the 2012–2050 period and would require regulated entities to hold rights, or allowances, to emit greenhouse gases. After allowances were initially distributed, entities would be free to buy and sell them (the trade part of the program). Those entities that emit more gases face a higher cost, which provides an economic incentive to reduce emissions. Key elements of the bill include:[47]

- Requires electric utilities to meet 20% of their electricity demand through renewable energy sources and energy efficiency by 2020.
- Subsidizes new clean energy technologies and energy efficiency, including renewable energy ($90 billion in new subsidies by 2025), carbon capture and sequestration ($60 billion), electric and other advanced technology vehicles ($20 billion), and basic scientific research and development ($20 billion).
- Protects consumers from energy price increases. According to estimates from the Environmental Protection Agency, the reductions in carbon pollution required by the legislation will cost American families less than a postage stamp per day (about $13.20 a month, and $160.60 a year).
- It sets a slightly higher target for reductions in emissions of carbon dioxide, methane, and other greenhouse gases than that proposed by President Barack Obama. The bill requires a 17-percent emissions reduction from 2005 levels by 2020; Obama has proposed a 14 percent reduction by 2020. Both plans would reduce United States' emissions by about 83 percent by 2050. Complementary measures in the legislation, such as efforts to prevent tropical deforestation, will achieve significant additional reductions in carbon emissions.
- It includes a renewable electricity standard (almost identical to a renewable portfolio standard, but narrowly tailored to electrical energy) requiring each electricity provider who supplies over 4 million megawatt hours (MWh) to produce 20 percent of its electricity from renewable sources (such as wind, solar,

---

[47] Et al

and geothermal) by 2020. There is a provision whereby 5% of this standard can be met through energy efficiency savings, as well as an additional 3% with certification of the Governor of the state in which the provider operates.
Alternative compliance payments are $25/MWh in violation of the standard, adjusted for inflation beginning in 2010.

- It provides for modernization of the electrical grid
- It provides for expanded production of electric vehicles and other advanced automobile technology.
- It mandates significant increases in energy efficiency in buildings, home appliances, and electricity generation.

The bill's cap-and-trade program allocates 85% of allowances to industry for free, auctioning the remainder.[48] The revenue from these allowances will be used to finance conservation of tropical forests abroad and to support low-income households.[49] The key word here is *revenue*. The crafters of the legislation see the *value* of clean air. They believe you will support them in monetizing it. That is to say, if the professional voter will support the taxation of the air of the rich in order to get a larger check, they will accomplish their main objective. What is that objective? Ah, the best is yet to come, so keep reading.

30% of the allowances will be allocated directly to local distribution companies (LDCs) who are mandated to use them exclusively for the benefit of customers. 5% will go to merchant coal generators and others with long-term power purchase agreements.[50] In short, everyone along the way gets to share a small portion of the spoils, except the shareholders of the companies who generate and distribute the electricity.

There is a new crack in the wall of the EPA. The Supreme Court ruled on Wednesday, March 21st of 2012 that landowners can sue to challenge an EPA compliance order under the clean water law, a decision that sides

---

[48] Stone, Andy (2009-06-24). "A Winner In The New Climate Legislation".*Forbes*. Retrieved 2009-07-04.
[49] Tropical Forest Conservation in Waxman Markey". Stevenson, Andrew. June 9, 2009. Retrieved August 28, 2009.
[50] Summary-House of Representatives-July 2009

with corporate groups and puts new limits on a key Environmental Protection Agency power. The justices unanimously rejected the government's position that individuals or companies must first fail to comply with an EPA order and face potentially costly enforcement action before a court can review the case.

The opinion by Justice Antonin Scalia was a victory for an Idaho couple who challenged a 2007 EPA order that required them to restore a wetland they had filled with dirt and rock as they began to build a new vacation home near Priest Lake. They were also told to stop construction on the home.

The couple, Chantell and Michael Sackett, denied their property had ever contained a wetland and complained they were being forced to comply with an order without a court hearing. Their appeal drew support from the Chamber of Commerce, the National Association of Manufacturers, the National Association of Home Builders and General Electric Co, a company that had made a similar challenge to the EPA compliance orders.[51]

Yes, you heard correctly. The mighty General Electric fought the EPA and lost. If you are thinking of a career, you might try focusing on honing your skills as an EPA dragon slayer. I imagine there will be tremendous opportunity in dismantling the Empire Protection Agency's crystal castle.

State Sovereignty and Federal Tax Funds Act

Such laws would require that all federal taxes come first to the state's Department of Revenue. A panel of legislators would assay the Constitutional appropriateness of the Federal Budget, and then forward to the federal government a percentage of the federal tax dollars that are delineated as legal and Constitutionally-justified. The remainder of those dollars would be assigned to budgetary items that are currently funded through federal allocations and grants or returned to the people of the state. The logic is that by circumventing the Federal handling charges, which

---

[51] "U.S. top court backs landowners, limits power of EPA" Reuters March 21, 2012 by James Vicini

currently sit at about 43 cents on every dollar, the entire process will become more efficient.

There is a very good example of what will happen when this Act becomes State law. Let's compare the Federal government's current requirement to be first in line for tax dollars collected by the States with the national unions. Here is the core issue.

Government employees include teachers, fire fighters, police, and dozens of other functions. Some states are classified *right-to-work* and others are completely unionized. That is to say, in some states a teacher or a fire fighter can hold employment without belonging to the union, and in some states union membership is mandatory. Of course, union membership doesn't come cheaply.

Each union member must pay dues to the union on a monthly basis. In some states, the employer collects the union dues from the paycheck just like it does social security or other taxes and then distributes those dues to the union. The employee never really notices the money is paid, and usually just pays attention to the net amount on the check.

In Wisconsin, Governor Scott Walker was facing huge budget deficits and needed a way to alleviate the financial burden. He did what any good CEO does. He examined labor costs. What he found was a half-century long trail of compromises made by previous executive officers to the government employee unions. There were numerous areas where the government employee was receiving expensive benefits far beyond those of the private sector, all at the taxpayer's expense.

In order to save his State from bankruptcy and honor his commitment to serve the taxpayers of Wisconsin, he decided to ask the legislators to draft some changes to the employment practice.

Although the Wisconsin Budget Repair Bill made changes in medical benefits, protections from firing and disciplinary actions, and other budgetary adjustments, the main prize was the impact on what the unions carefully couch as *collective bargaining rights*. It isn't the right to bargain

131

as a group with the employer that is placed in jeopardy. It is one very simple process that makes them realize their glory days are over.

The bill would make various changes to limit collective bargaining for most public employees to wages. Employers would be prohibited from collecting union dues and members of collective bargaining units would not be required to pay dues. Local law enforcement and fire employees, and state troopers and inspectors would be exempt from these changes[52]

This means two things. First, the employee would have to write their own union dues check to the union. Second, if the employee decided they could use those union dues somewhere else, they did not lose their job. The unions are furious and have marshaled their political arm, the Democrat Party, for a civil war.

The Democrats tried several tactics. They expressed solidarity with their bosses and left town to stop the legislation by denying the legislation a quorum. The remaining legislators voted anyway and passed the Bill. They ordered union employees from national resources to descend on the State capital of Wisconsin to protest the Bill and ask for Governor Walker to resign.

As of the writing of this book, the Democrats have created and received the proper signatures for a recall election of Governor Walker. After the mandatory 12 months of his term have passed, which is right now, the election will be held. The unions have selected and polished a few politicians they can control more completely to run against Mr. Walker in the election.

The results so far are nothing short of stunning. Governor Walker's strategy has been successful. The State has a balanced budget, the debt is coming down, and no government services have been negatively impacted. Of course, the union has lost thousands of members. The citizens of Wisconsin are now free to choose whether to pay the cost and belong to the union or not.

---

[52] Governor Scott Walker (2011-02-11). "Governor Walker Introduces Budget Repair". Office of the Governor. State of Wisconsin.

Exactly the same thing will happen when the States choose to place themselves first in the chart of accounts for Federal taxes collected in their State. The dollars will be used more effectively without a negative impact on government services, and the Federal government will go to war by descending upon the State houses with everything they have.

Guess Who's Coming to Dinar?

August 2nd, 1990 Iraq invaded Kuwait and absconded with cash and gold and claimed Kuwait as Iraqi territory. Three days later, President George Bush stated that the Iraqi invasion would not stand. The Kuwaiti Dinar was taken off the world market and declared a stolen currency, with exception of the locally held currency and that which was legitimately purchased. Very few people knew what to do at the time. The rest of the world was transformed into news junkies as *news at eleven* became a 24-hour a day newscast called CNN. While we could not take our eyes off the world's first and greatest reality program, the currency barons were behind the scenes staging for a trillion-dollar currency deal.

On June 8th, 1991, less than a year later, the victory parade was held in Washington, DC. A new Kuwaiti Dinar was issued, and legitimate currency was traded for the new currency. The Kuwaiti dinar increased in value to be worth $3.40 USD in a period of ten years. Had an investor had the foresight to invest $1,000.00 USD in 1991 they would have $3.3 million USD today.

Enter the Iraq War. Would be investors who missed the boat last time are trying to cash in on the opportunity. Does the Iraqi Dinar have similar potential? That's what everyone wants to know.

Lords of Finance: The Bankers Who Broke the World by Liaquat Ahamed is about how the four leading central bankers from the U.S., U.K., France and Germany navigated in and out of WWI and financed recoveries and German reparations. These central bankers went off and on the gold and new dollar standards by manipulating their exchange and interest rates and much more. It was a world steeped in insider trading and special knowledge that allowed financial powerhouses to manipulate the military-industrial complex to virtually enslave the entire world in a matrix of debt.

This is how money and power (military and otherwise) go hand in hand. Global dominance today is based upon the profits made during that war. In fact, as has already been stated in this book, the only thing the folks down at Wars-R-Us are not prepared for is the absence of war; also known as peace. It is one thing to be safe, and it is quite another to be all dressed up and have no one to kill.

The US Treasury estimates that 2+ million Americans own the Iraqi Dinar. These small investors own this investment for one reason; to make a windfall profit when the Iraqi Dinar goes back on the market at the new value. Iraq as a sovereign country must revalue its currency. There is an enormous war debt to repay. There are capital improvements they need to make in their own country. Iraq has in its possession the 2rd largest oil reserves in the world, and they have an almost unique ability to become the shining Democracy in the Middle East with streets paved with gold and clean water for everyone. The Bush administration did set this entire plan up which is fashioned after his father's Kuwaiti dinar revalue back in 1993.

Would the revaluation benefit the USA? The capital gains taxes AND the FACT that the US Treasury has in its possession approximately 3-5 trillion Iraqi Dinar indicate that this is not a scam. That is, unless it is being perpetrated by the Administration on the American people.

There are several differences that make this entire opportunity irresistible. First, the Iraqi economy is many times larger than the Kuwaiti economy, so there is much more currency in circulation than the Kuwaiti Dinar. Second, the currency held by millions of Americans, and even more around the world, was not stolen. Legitimate Iraqi notes were purchased for about $0.001 per Dinar. Third, the largest owner of the dormant currency is the U.S. Treasury.

Did the Bush administration plan on, and is the Obama administration still considering, paying for part or all of the Iraq war by collecting taxes from the revaluation of the dinar? You can take that to the bank.

Historically the Iraqi Dinar has always been around three or four dollars to the Dinar, and this is the hope that many investors in the United States have; that once again the Dinar will reach this status. The Federal Reserve supposedly has trillions of dinars as well. The leaders of Iraq have promised the people of Iraq that the dinar will reach the levels it once held and this has further emboldened Americans to know that their investment will pay vast dividends. Hardly a week goes by that the Iraqi press does not discuss progress made toward this end.

President Obama signed into law the right for American Citizens to buy Dinars, and currently the discussion is that Americans will pay 15% of their return to the government in taxes. There is no tax loophole for currency trading. Currently Americans own roughly 3 trillion dinars. If the Dinar revalues to a rate of 3 dollars per dinar, this will lead to about 9 trillion dollars in new revenue that Americans have, 15% of which would go directly to the US government. This does not include the billions that these men and women would spend on goods and services that would lead to a boost to the economy and more jobs for our citizens. The businesses from which they purchase all this stuff also must pay taxes on the revenue. You get the picture.

Will the U.S. Treasury allow millions of average Americans who made legitimate investments in currency to reap the same profits as they take from the exchange? The answer is that it does not matter much. In the grand scheme of things, if the U.S. Treasury reaps the profits they planned, the American debt could be reduced by as much as 50% whether or not the average little investor gets to trade his currency. After all, what is one more loss of $5,000 to your life savings? Nothing. It will be infuriating to not be able to turn that into $15 million, but it won't be the end of the world if it turns out that only the government gets to cash in. Heaven help them at the ballot box if that happens, but hear me out.

What will be the effects of this? I'm glad you asked that question. Let me begin to answer the question with a question. Who owns most of the American debt? China. China's economy is the second fastest growing economy in the world, behind only India, and it is largely fueled by two things.

First, China's currency is held artificially at a low fixed value by their government. This means that foreign investment in their country is easy, and the sale of Chinese goods is even easier. How do they make up the difference in value? You guessed it. The interest paid to them on the American debt. After all, what better hedge is there than bonds backed by the faith and credit of the United States of America? Well, there is a way to reduce the yield on those bonds by about 75%. Pay them off. The Chinese economy may implode as free market forces will demand growth, but there will be no capital to fuel it. That giant sucking sound we heard when all our jobs went to China may sound like the south end of a horse that's eaten too much Alfalfa. Once people taste of prosperity, it cannot be jerked away without the teeth coming after you in the process.

If the U.S. Treasury pays off the American debt held by China, it will collapse their economy. The U.S will be out of the deficit business unless someone goes absolutely hog wild with new government spending. Yeah, like that has ever happened before. I hope it doesn't make the planners at Wars-R-Us book flights for the Far East.

Second, the capital at the banks that had been loaned out to the U.S. government will now be back in the cash drawer so to speak. This will be panic time for the major banks. Without the money falling from heaven paid to them by the interest on U.S. debt, they will be in a lending crisis. Who is going to borrow all that money and make payments? What are they going to do with all that cash?

Enter, U.S. small business. With the U.S. government out of the borrowing business, because the budget better damned well be balanced from here on out, there will be capital to lend. The credit will be extended to American business to expand, hiring people; lot's of people. Working people spend money to buy things. The economic tiger will be out of the cage, and it will be up to the skills of Mr. Bernanke to tame it. Interest rates will skyrocket in an attempt to curb what they perceive as inflation. Actually, everyone knows there is only one thing that causes inflation. Government printing money.

The fact that people are working and paying taxes, and buying stuff and paying taxes, and paying off their own debts means that the economy is going to grow. Growth is not inflation.

There is one more thing. If President Obama agrees to allow the Iraqi Dinar to revaluate, and he allows American investors, both large and small, to cash in on this revaluation, it will be the windfall he has been looking for. The unemployment rate will drop to less than 5%. The national debt will be cut in half, and the budget will be balanced. The banks will be lending again, letting small business back into the economy, which will add about one million jobs per month.

Mark my words. If this occurs, Republicans will not get within a thousand miles of the White House, and may lose the House as well. President Obama will be the Democrat of the century. Now, if the Democrats know this, and now you know it, there is a 50% chance the Republicans know it, too. So is it Obama who is holding back the economy, or is it the Republicans who will not allow this to happen on his watch?

Again, the alienation of America is facilitated by the greed and lust of men for power. I encourage you to pay close attention to the events between May and October of 2012. The Presidential election will start the first Tuesday after Labor Day, 2012. If the revaluated Iraqi Dinar is allowed to trade, President Obama will win.

Perhaps part of the alienation of the nation is that the people who would like to see the Democrats lose this election are also the ones who stand to personally gain from the entire Iraqi Dinar Caper to succeed. It's alright, I suppose, if every bird flies into the sights of their gun, but not their neighbor's, too. Interesting sociological quandary, wouldn't you say?

"I guess the revolution has arrived in Virginia, and I am
delighted that I was here. It's very appropriate that the
state of Virginia be involved in our revolution that's going
on. Of course, our revolution is the American Revolution.
We had a pretty good start in this country a few years
back, but we drifted away and for many years now, for
nearly a hundred years, I think there's been a lot of
forgetting of what the original intent of the constitution
was, They have forgotten what a true republic is all about.
That is our goal, to restore the American republic to the
American people."[53] –Ron Paul

While I was writing this book I felt the surge of patriotism inside of me the
founding fathers must have felt as they were considering the Declaration
of Independence and arguing their way through the Articles of the
Constitution. I could see their passion in the words, "We hold these truths
to be self-evident..."

Aristotle once said that all knowledge is innate. That is to say, if you sat in
meditation long enough about a certain subject, the truth will come to you
from your own self. I think, as do billions of other sentient beings that
have lived on this and other planets, that the higher self is intimately
involved in these epiphanies. The definition of *innate* is, "inherent in the
essential character of something; existing in one from birth."

When Thomas Jefferson sat down, allegedly alone, to pen the Declaration
of Independence there were no cross-outs. There were no erasures. There
was no shadow of a mistake in that parchmented work of literature. Was
this great knowledge innate within Mr. Jefferson? I think not.

It is my belief that there was a design, older than America will be in the
next millennium, that was folded up in the soul of man himself. This
design was a form of self-government that would allow the human race to

---

[53] Congressman Dr. Ron Paul speech to gathering in Virginia Feb 28, 2012

reach the fullness of its potential using principles of the Republic he penned in that chamber. There is also evident another design that is perhaps even older.

There is another design that is supported by the weak and unempowered masses. It was designed by beings whose desire is to lead sheep and not shepherds. It was designed to keep a few men soaking drunk in the wealth of others while providing only enough to those dependents to keep them hoping for another few crumbs. There would be no dreaming. There would be no mechanism for self-reliance. The breadwinner would be completely replaced by their government, emasculating the males and effectively removing them from society. Once they are removed and obfuscated, they cannot threaten the leadership of the government, because the females would be completely addicted to the welfare State.

In this form of agency-government, there would be no available resource for an entrepreneur to be germinated. The driving force of the self-will of the individual to grow and provide opportunity for employment for the many without the aid of government would be absolutely forbidden under this form of government. There is no possibility for freedom and liberty. This system of subterfuge has been built many times upon the Earth and perhaps on other worlds and in other times. The modus is to request that the people abdicate their own liberty to their leaders in exchange for a promise of security. The people always happily comply. Some people still think there is such a thing as a free lunch. Unfortunately for democracies, these very same people are also voters who perpetuate the eradication of liberty.

History has shown us that this system of government tends to stagnate. That is to say, the stream of commerce and opportunity is dammed up. Ideas and innovations that might compete against the interests of the Federal government are denied access to capital. The population that makes up the pool of stagnating water begins to separate, like water and salad oil.

What happens then is both extraordinary and predictable. The State tax revenue begins to drain to the Federal government. States that do not have

140

a Federal interest lose money. States that have Federal interests take in more money than they send to the Federal government.

This is precisely what precipitated the War Between the States. You may have never read this before. These are the words of South Carolina making its case for secession from the Library of Congress:

"In the year 1765, that portion of the British Empire embracing Great Britain, undertook to make laws for the government of that portion composed of the thirteen American Colonies. A struggle for the right of self-government ensued, which resulted, on the 4th of July, 1776, in a Declaration, by the Colonies, "that they are, and of right ought to be, FREE AND INDEPENDENT STATES; and that, as free and independent States, they have full power to levy war, conclude peace, contract alliances, establish commerce, and to do all other acts and things which independent States may of right do."
They further solemnly declared that whenever any "form of government becomes destructive of the ends for which it was established, it is the right of the people to alter or abolish it, and to institute a new government."
Deeming the Government of Great Britain to have become destructive of these ends, they declared that the Colonies "are absolved from all allegiance to the British Crown, and that all political connection between them and the State of Great Britain is, and ought to be, totally dissolved.
"In pursuance of this Declaration of Independence, each of the thirteen States proceeded to exercise its separate sovereignty; adopted for itself a Constitution, and appointed officers for the administration of government in all its departments-- Legislative, Executive and Judicial. For purposes of defense, they united their arms and their counsels; and, in 1778, they entered into a League known as the Articles of Confederation, whereby they agreed to entrust the administration of their external relations to a

common agent, known as the Congress of the United States, expressly declaring, in the first Article "that each State retains its sovereignty, freedom and independence, and every power, jurisdiction and right which is not, by this Confederation, expressly delegated to the United States in Congress assembled."[54]

Mississippi had similar contemplations and a commitment to Secession. These are words of passion. Some of the text of their statement refers to the practice of slavery; however, this is not the subject that I wish to address with this book and is redacted to preserve the idea of State's rights while not inciting the prejudgment of the reader. Slavery is abhorrent in all its forms, whether to own another human being or to subjugate him so the commands of debt for a lifetime without hope of deliverance.

> "It (the Federal government) has invaded a State, and invested with the honors of martyrdom the wretch whose purpose was to apply flames to our dwellings, and the weapons of destruction to our lives.
> It has broken every compact into which it has entered for our security.
> It has given indubitable evidence of its design to ruin our agriculture, to prostrate our industrial pursuits and to destroy our social system.
> It knows no relenting or hesitation in its purposes; it stops not in its march of aggression, and leaves us no room to hope for cessation or for pause.
> It has recently obtained control of the Government, by the prosecution of its unhallowed schemes, and destroyed the last expectation of living together in friendship and brotherhood.
> Utter subjugation awaits us in the Union, if we should consent longer to remain in it. It is not a matter of choice, but of necessity. We must either submit to degradation, and to the loss of property worth four billions of money,

---

[54] Library of Congress J.A. May & J.R. Faunt, *South Carolina Secedes* (U. of S. Car. Pr, 1960), pp. 76-81

or we must secede from the Union framed by our fathers, to secure this as well as every other species of property. For far less cause than this, our fathers separated from the Crown of England.

Our decision is made. We follow their footsteps. We embrace the alternative of separation; and for the reasons here stated, we resolve to maintain our rights with the full consciousness of the justice of our course, and the undoubting belief of our ability to maintain it."[55]

Georgia, whose State flag was once the flag of the capitol of the Confederacy, made a factual case for secession as follows:

"The main reason was that the North, even if united, could not control both branches of the Legislature during any portion of that time. Therefore such an organization must have resulted either in utter failure or in the total overthrow of the Government. The material prosperity of the North was greatly dependent on the Federal Government; that of the South not at all. In the first years of the Republic the navigating, commercial, and manufacturing interests of the North began to seek profit and aggrandizement at the expense of the agricultural interests. Even the owners of fishing smacks sought and obtained bounties for pursuing their own business (which yet continue), and $500,000 is now paid them annually out of the Treasury. The navigating interests begged for protection against foreign shipbuilders and against competition in the coasting trade. Congress granted both requests, and by prohibitory acts gave an absolute monopoly of this business to each of their interests, which they enjoy without diminution to this day. Not content with these great and unjust advantages, they have sought to throw the legitimate burden of their business as much as possible upon the public; they have succeeded in throwing

---

[55] Library of Congress *"Journal of the State Convention"*, (Jackson, MS: E. Barksdale, State Printer, 1861), pp. 86-88

the cost of light-houses, buoys, and the maintenance of their seamen upon the Treasury, and the Government now pays above $2,000,000 annually for the support of these objects.

Thess interests, in connection with the commercial and manufacturing classes, have also succeeded, by means of subventions to mail steamers and the reduction in postage, in relieving their business from the payment of about $7,000,000 annually, throwing it upon the public Treasury under the name of postal deficiency. The manufacturing interests entered into the same struggle early, and has clamored steadily for Government bounties and special favors. This interest was confined mainly to the Eastern and Middle non-Southern States. Wielding these great States it held great power and influence, and its demands were in full proportion to its power. The manufacturers and miners wisely based their demands upon special facts and reasons rather than upon general principles, and thereby mollified much of the opposition of the opposing interest. They pleaded in their favor the infancy of their business in this country, the scarcity of labor and capital, the hostile legislation of other countries toward them, the great necessity of their fabrics in the time of war, and the necessity of high duties to pay the debt incurred in our war for independence. These reasons prevailed, and they received for many years enormous bounties by the general acquiescence of the whole country.

But when these reasons ceased they were no less clamorous for Government protection, but their clamors were less heeded-- the country had put the principle of protection upon trial and condemned it. After having enjoyed protection to the extent of from 15 to 200 per cent. Upon their entire business for above thirty years, the act of 1846 was passed. It avoided sudden change, but the principle was settled, and free trade, low duties, and economy in public expenditures was the verdict of the American people. The South and the Northwestern States sustained this policy. There was but small hope of its reversal; upon the direct issue, none at all."

"...For forty years this question has been considered and debated in the halls of Congress, before the people, by the press, and before the tribunals of justice. The majority of the people of the North in 1860 decided it in their own favor. We refuse to submit to that judgment, and in vindication of our refusal we offer the Constitution of our country and point to the total absence of any express power to exclude us. We offer the practice of our Government for the first thirty years of its existence in complete refutation of the position that any such power is either necessary or proper to the execution of any other power in relation to the Territories. We offer the judgment of a large minority of the people of the North, amounting to more than one-third, who united with the unanimous voice of the South against this usurpation; and, finally, we offer the judgment of the Supreme Court of the United States, the highest judicial tribunal of our country, in our favor. This evidence ought to be conclusive that we have never surrendered this right. The conduct of our adversaries admonishes us that if we had surrendered it, it is time to resume it.

The faithless conduct of our adversaries is not confined to such acts as might aggrandize themselves or their section of the Union. They are content if they can only injure us. The Constitution declares that persons charged with crimes in one State and fleeing to another shall be delivered up on the demand of the executive authority of the State from which they may flee, to be tried in the jurisdiction where the crime was committed. It would appear difficult to employ language freer from ambiguity, yet for above twenty years the non-Southern States generally have wholly refused to deliver up to us persons charged with crimes affecting slave property. Our confederates, with punic faith, shield and give sanctuary to all criminals who seek to deprive us of this property or who use it to destroy us. This clause of the Constitution has no other sanction than their good faith; that is withheld from us; we are remediless in the Union; out of it we are remitted to the laws of nations." [56]

Texas, the only State not to sign the Reconstruction Agreements after the war was over, resolved that it would secede from the Union as well.

"The government of the United States, by certain joint resolutions, bearing date the 1st day of March, in the year A.D. 1845, proposed to the Republic of Texas, then *a free, sovereign and independent nation*, the annexation of the latter to the former, as one of the co-equal states thereof.

The people of Texas, by deputies in convention assembled, on the fourth day of July of the same year, assented to and accepted said proposals and formed a constitution for the proposed State, upon which on the 29th day of December in the same year, said State was formally admitted into the Confederated Union.

Texas abandoned her separate national existence and consented to become one of the Confederated Union to promote her welfare, insure domestic tranquility and secure more substantially the blessings of peace and liberty to her people. She was received into the confederacy with her own constitution, under the guarantee of the federal constitution and the compact of annexation, that she should enjoy these blessings....Her institutions and geographical position established the strongest ties between her and other Southern States of the confederacy. Those ties have been strengthened by association. But what has been the course of the government of the United States, and of the people and

---

[56] Library of Congress
Georgia Official Records, Ser IV, vol 1, pp. 81-85.

authorities of the non-Southern States, since our connection with them?

The controlling majority of the Federal Government, under various pretences and disguises, has so administered the same as to exclude the citizens of the Southern States, unless under odious and unconstitutional restrictions, from all the immense territory owned in common by all the States on the Pacific Ocean, for the avowed purpose of acquiring sufficient power in the common government to use it as a means of destroying the institutions of Texas and her sister States.

By the disloyalty of the Northern States and their citizens and the imbecility of the Federal Government, infamous combinations of incendiaries and outlaws have been permitted in those States and the common territory of Kansas to trample upon the federal laws, to war upon the lives and property of Southern citizens in that territory, and finally, by violence and mob law, to usurp the possession of the same as exclusively the property of the Northern States.

The Federal Government, while but partially under the control of these our unnatural and sectional enemies, has for years almost entirely failed to protect the lives and property of the people of Texas against the Indian savages on our border, and more recently against the murderous forays of banditti from the neighboring territory of Mexico; and when our State government has expended large amounts for such purpose, the Federal Government has refuse reimbursement therefore, thus rendering our condition more insecure and harassing than it was during the existence of the Republic of Texas.

These and other wrongs we have patiently borne in the vain hope that a returning sense of justice and humanity would induce a different course of administration.

When we advert to the course of individual non-Southern States, and that a majority of their citizens, our grievances assume far greater magnitude.

147

The States of Maine, Vermont, New Hampshire, Connecticut, Rhode Island, Massachusetts, New York, Pennsylvania, Ohio, Wisconsin, Michigan and Iowa, by solemn legislative enactments, have deliberately, directly or indirectly violated the 3rd clause of the 2nd section of the 4th article [the fugitive slave clause] of the federal constitution, and laws passed in pursuance thereof; thereby annulling a material provision of the compact, designed by its framers to perpetuate the amity between the members of the confederacy and to secure the rights of the Southern States in their domestic institutions-- a provision founded in justice and wisdom, and without the enforcement of which the compact fails to accomplish the object of its creation. Some of those States have imposed high fines and degrading penalties upon any of their citizens or officers who may carry out in good faith that provision of the compact, or the federal laws enacted in accordance therewith.

In all the non-Southern States, in violation of that good faith and comity which should exist between entirely distinct nations, the people have formed themselves into a great sectional party, now strong enough in numbers to control the affairs of each of those States...

By consolidating their strength, they have placed the Southern States in a hopeless minority in the federal congress, and rendered representation of no avail in protecting Southern rights against their exactions and encroachments.

They have proclaimed, and at the ballot box sustained, the revolutionary doctrine that there is a 'higher law' than the constitution and laws of our Federal Union, and virtually that they will disregard their oaths and trample upon our rights.

They have for years past encouraged and sustained lawless organizations to steal our property and prevent its recovery, and have repeatedly murdered Southern citizens while lawfully seeking their rendition.

They have invaded Southern soil and murdered unoffending citizens, and through the press their leading men and a fanatical pulpit have bestowed praise upon the actors and assassins in these crimes, while the governors of several of their States have refused to deliver parties implicated and indicted for participation in such offenses, upon the legal demands of the States aggrieved.

They have, through the mails and hired emissaries, sent seditious pamphlets and papers among us to stir up servile insurrection and bring blood and carnage to our firesides.

They have sent hired emissaries among us to burn our towns and distribute arms to fuel their interests inside our community for the same purpose.

They have impoverished the Southern States by unequal and partial legislation, thereby enriching themselves by draining our substance.

They have refused to vote appropriations for protecting Texas against ruthless savages, for the sole reason that she is a Southern State.

And, finally, by the combined sectional vote of the seventeen non-Southern States, they have elected as president and vice-president of the whole confederacy two men whose chief claims to such high positions are their approval of these long continued wrongs, and their pledges to continue them to the final consummation of these schemes for the ruin of the Southern States."[57]

As I stated earlier, the quotation has been altered by me to remove the references to slavery as this is not the idea behind the motion to secede, and it is certainly not pertinent to the division of the States from the Union. The leaders of the Union made the case for war based upon the social issues of the day, while the economics of the entire debacle was not mentioned outside the pleadings of the Southern States that were being taxed and levied with tariffs by a Federal government spending like drunken sailors on every whim of the Northern States.

---

[57] Library of Congress E.W. Winkler, ed., *Journal of the Secession Convention of Texas,* pp. 61-66.

Finally, you must read the entire edited address of Robert Barnwell Rhett to the people assembled in Convention of the Southern States. This one State has led this nation into both of it revolutions. The passion and power of its statesmen have inspired other nations around the world for over a century. You can close your eyes and hear the powerful and regal southern accent and the oratory must have been such that within three years, the action was taken to evict Union troops from all Southern territory.

"It is now seventy-three years since the union between the United States was made by the Constitution of the United States. During this period their advance in wealth, prosperity, and power, has been with scarcely a parallel in the history of the world. The great object of their union was external defense from the aggressions of more powerful nations; now complete, from their more progress in power, thirty-one millions of people, with a commerce and navigation which explores every sea, and of agricultural productions which are necessary to every civilized people, command the friendship of the world.

But, unfortunately, our internal peace has not grown with our external prosperity. Discontent and contention has moved in the bosom of the Confederacy for the last thirty-five years. During this time South Carolina has twice called her people together in solemn convention, to take into consideration the aggressions and unconstitutional wrongs perpetrated by the people of the North on the people of the South. These wrongs were submitted to by the people of the South, under the hope and expectation that they would be final. But these hopes and expectations have proved to be void. Instead of being incentives to forbearance, our submission has only instigated to new forms of aggressions and outrage, and South Carolina, again assembling her people in convention, has this day dissolved her connection with the States constituting the United States.

The one great evil from which all other evils have flowed, is the overthrow of the Constitution of the United States. The Government of the United States is no longer the government of a confederate republic, but of a consolidated democracy. It is no longer a free government, but a despotism. It is, in fact, such a government as Great Britain attempted to set over our fathers, and which was resisted and defeated by a seven years struggle for independence.

The revolution of 1776 turned upon one great principle, self-government, and self-taxation the criterion of self-government. Where the interests of two people united together under one Government are different, each must have the power to protect its interests by the organization of the Government, or they cannot be free.

The interests of Great Britain and of the colonies were different and antagonistic. Great Britain was desirous of carrying out the policy of all nations toward their colonies of making them tributary to their wealth and power. She had vast and complicated relations with the whole world. Her policy toward her North American colonies was to identify them with her in all these complicated relations, and to make them bear, in common with the rest of the empire, the full burden of her obligations and necessities. She had a vast public debt; she had a European policy and an Asiatic policy, which had occasioned the accumulation of her public debt, and which kept her in continual wars.

The North American colonies saw their interests, political and commercial, sacrificed by such a policy. Their interests required that they should not be identified with the burdens and wars of the mother country. They had been settled under charters which gave them self-government, at least so far as their property was concerned. They had taxed themselves, and had never been taxed by the Government of Great Britain. To make them a part of a consolidated empire the Parliament of Great Britain determined to assume the power of legislating for the colonies in all cases whatsoever. Our ancestors resisted the pretension. They refused to be a part of the consolidated Government of Great Britain.

The Southern States now stand exactly in the same position toward the Northern States that our ancestors in the colonies did toward Great Britain. The Northern States, having the majority in Congress, claim the same power of omnipotence in legislation as the British Parliament. "The general welfare" is the only limit to the legislation of either; and the majority in Congress, as in the British Parliament, are the sole judges of the expediency of the legislation this "general welfare" requires. Thus the Government of the United States has become a consolidated Government, and the people of the Southern States are compelled to meet the very despotism their fathers threw off in the Revolution of 1776.

The consolidation of the Government of Great Britain over the colonies was attempted to be carried out by the taxes. The British Parliament undertook to tax the colonies to promote British interests. Our fathers resisted this pretension. They claimed the right of self-taxation through their Colonial Legislatures. They were not represented in the British Parliament, and therefore could not rightfully be taxed by its Legislature. The British Government, however, offered them a representation in the British Parliament; but it was not sufficient to enable them to protect themselves from the majority, and they refused it.

Between taxation without any representation, and taxation without a representation adequate to protection, there was no difference. By neither would the colonies tax themselves. Hence they refused to pay the taxes paid by the British Parliament.

The Southern States now stand in the same relation toward the Northern States, in the vital matter of taxation, that our ancestors stood toward the people of Great Britain. They are in a minority in Congress. Their representation in Congress is useless to protect them against unjust taxation, and they are taxed by the people of the North for their benefit exactly as the people of Great Britain taxed our ancestors in the British Parliament for their benefit. For the last forty years the taxes laid by the Congress of the United States have been laid with a view of subserving the interests of the North. The people of the South have been taxed by duties on imports not for revenue, but for an object inconsistent with revenue -- to promote, by prohibitions, Northern interests in the productions of their mines and manufactures.

There is another evil in the condition of the Southern toward the Northern States, which our ancestors refused to bear toward Great Britain. Our ancestors not only taxed themselves, but all the taxes collected from them were expended among them. Had they submitted to the pretensions of the British Government, the taxes collected from them would have been expended on other parts of the British Empire. They were fully aware of the effect of such a policy in impoverishing the people from whom taxes are collected, and in enriching those who receive the benefit of their expenditure. To prevent the evils of such a policy was one of the motives which drove them on to revolution.

"Yet this British policy has been fully realized toward the Southern States by the Northern States. The people of the Southern States are not only taxed for the benefit of the Northern States, but after the taxes are collected three-fourths of them are expended at the North. This cause, with others connected with the operation of the General Government, has provincialized the cities of the South. Their growth is paralyzed, while they are the mere suburbs of Northern cities. The bases of the foreign commerce of the United States are the agricultural productions of the South; yet Southern cities do not carry it on. Our foreign trade is almost annihilated. In 1740 there were five shipyards in South Carolina to build ships to carry on our direct trade with Europe. Between 1740 and 1779 there were built in these yards twenty-five square-rigged vessels, beside a great number of sloops and schooners to carry on our coast and West India trade. In the half century immediately preceding the Revolution, from 1725 to 1775, the population of South Carolina increased seven-fold.

No man can for a moment believe that our ancestors intended to establish over their posterity exactly the same sort of Government they had overthrown. The great object of the Constitution of the United States, in its internal operation, was, doubtless, to secure the great end of the Revolution -- a limited free Government -- a Government limited to those matters only which were general and common to all portions of the United States. All sectional or local interests were to be left to the States. By no other arrangement would they obtain free government by a Constitution common to so vast a Confederacy. Yet, by gradual and steady encroachments on the part of the North, and submission on the part of the South, the limitations in the Constitution have been swept away, and the Government of the United States has become consolidated, with a claim of limitless powers in its operations.

It is not at all surprising, while such is the character of the Government of the United States, that it should assume to possess power over all the institutions of the country. The agitations on the subject of Slavery in the South are the natural results of the consolidation of the Government. Responsibility follows power; and if the people of the North have the power by Congress "to promote the general welfare of the United States," by any means they deem expedient, why should they not assail and overthrow the institution of Slavery in the South? They are responsible for its continuance or existence, in proportion to their power. A majority in Congress, according to their interested and perverted views, is omnipotent. The inducements to act upon the subject of Slavery, under such circumstances, were so imperious as to amount almost to a moral necessity. To make, however, their numerical power available to rule the Union, the North must consolidate their power. It would not be united on any matter common to the whole Union -- in other words, on any constitutional subject -- for on such subjects divisions are as likely to exist in the North as in the South.

Slavery was strictly a sectional interest. If this could be made the criterion of parties at the North, the North could be united in its power, and thus carry out its measures of sectional ambition, encroachment, and aggrandizement. To build up their sectional predominance in the Union, the Constitution must be first abolished by constructions; but that being done, the consolidation of the North to rule the South, by the tariff and Slavery issues, was in the obvious course of things.

The Constitution of the United States was an experiment. The experiment consisted in uniting under one Government different peoples, living in different climates, and having different pursuits of industry and institutions. It matters not how carefully the limitations of such a government are laid down in the constitution -- its success must at least depend upon the good faith of the parties to the constitutional compact in enforcing them. It is not in the power of human language to exclude false inferences, constructions, and perversions, in any constitution; and when vast sectional interests are to be subserved involving the appropriation of countless millions of money it has not been the usual experience of mankind that words on parchment can arrest power.

The Constitution of the United States, irrespective of the interposition of the States, rested on the assumption that power would yield to faith -- that integrity would be stronger than interest, and that thus the limitations of the Constitution would be observed. The experiment has been fairly made. The Southern States, from the commencement of the Government, have striven to keep it within the orbit prescribed by the Constitution. The experiment has failed. The whole Constitution by the constructions of the Northern people, has been swallowed up by a few words in its preamble. In their reckless lust for power they seem unable to comprehend that seeming parado. That the more power is given to the General Government the weaker it becomes. Its strength consists in its generality and limitations. To extend the scope of its power over sectional or local interests is to raise up against it opposition and resistance. In all such matters the General Government must necessarily be a despotism, because all sectional or local interests must ever be represented by a minority in the councils of the General Government -- having no power to protect itself against the rule of the majority. The majority, constituted from those who do not represent these sectional or local interests, will control and govern them.

A free people cannot submit to such a Government; and the more it enlarges the sphere of its power the greater must be the dissatisfaction it must produce, and the weaker it must become. On the contrary, the more it abstains from usurped powers, and the more faithfully it adheres to the limitations of the Constitution, the stronger it is made. The Northern people have had neither the wisdom nor the faith to perceive that to observe the limitation of the Constitution was the only way to its perpetuity.

Under such a Government there must, of course, be many and endless "irrepressible conflicts," between the two great sections of the Union. The same faithlessness which has abolished the Constitution of the United States, will not fail to carry out the sectional purposes for which it has been abolished.

There must be conflict; and the weaker section of the Union can only find peace and liberty in an independence of the North. The repeated efforts made by South

Carolina, in a wise conservatism, to arrest the progress of the General Government in its fatal progress to consolidation, have been unsupported and denounced as faithless to the obligations of the Constitution by the very men and States who were destroying it by their usurpations. It is now too late to reform or restore the Government of the United States. All confidence in the North is lost in the South. The faithlessness of half a century has opened a gulf of separation between them which no promises or engagements can fill.

It cannot be believed that our ancestors would have assented to any union whatever with the people of the North if the feelings and opinions now existing among them had existed when the Constitution was framed. There was then no tariff... It was the delegates from New England who proposed in the Convention which framed the Constitution, to the delegates from South Carolina and Georgia, that if they would agree to give Congress the power of regulating commerce by a majority, that they would support the extension of the *Southern foreign trade* for twenty years. *Foreign trade* existed in all the States but one.

The idea that they would be made to pay that tribute to their Northern confederates which they had refused to pay to Great Britain, or that the institution of *foreign trade* would be made the grand basis of a sectional organization of the North to rule the South, never crossed their imaginations.... They were guilty of no such folly.

Time and the progress of things have totally altered the relations between the Northern and Southern States since the Union was first established. That identity of feeling, interests, and institutions which once existed is gone. They are now divided between agricultural and manufacturing and commercial States -- between Southern and Northern States. Their institutions and industrial pursuits have made them totally different peoples. That equality in the Government between the two sections of the Union which once existed, no longer exists. We but imitate the policy of our fathers in dissolving a union with Northern confederates, and seeking a confederation with Southern States.

Experience has proved that Southern States cannot be safe in subjection to Northern States. Indeed, no people ever expect to preserve their rights and liberties unless they are in their own custody. To plunder and oppress where plunder and oppression can be practiced with impunity, seems to be the natural order of things. The fairest portions of the world have been turned into wildernesses, and the most civilized and prosperous communities have been impoverished and ruined by fanaticism.

The people of the North have not left us in doubt as to their designs and policy. United as a section in the late Presidential election, they have elected as the exponent of their policy one who has openly declared that all the States of the United States must be *subjected to the rule of the Union...* And when it is considered that the Northern States will soon have the power to make the Supreme Court what they please, and that the Constitution has never been any barrier whatever to their exercise of power, what check can there be in the unrestrained councils of the North?

There is sympathy in association, which carries men along without principle; but when there is principle, and that principle is fortified by long existing prejudices and feelings, association is omnipotent in party influences. The hypocrisy of thirty years -- the faithlessness of their whole course from the commencement of our union with them -- show that the people of the North are not and cannot be safe associates of the South under a common Government. Not only their fanaticism, but their erroneous views of the principles of free governments, render it doubtful whether, separated from the South, they can maintain a free Government among themselves. Brute numbers with them is the great element of free Government. A majority is infallible and omnipotent.

"The right divine to rule in kings," is only transferred to their majority. The very object of all constitutions, in free, popular Governments, is to restrain the majority. Constitutions, therefore, according to their theory, must be most unrighteous inventions, restricting liberty. None ought to exist, but the body politic ought simply to have a political organization, to bring out and enforce the will of a majority.

This theory may be harmless in a small community, having an identity of interests and pursuits, but over a vast State -- still more, over a vast Confederacy, having various and conflicting interests and pursuits -- it is a remorseless despotism. In resisting it, as applicable to ourselves, we are vindicating the great cause of free government, more important, perhaps, to the world than the existence of the United States. Nor in resisting it, do we intend to depart from the safe instrumentality the system of government we have established with them requires.

In separating from them we invade no rights -- no interest of theirs. We violate no obligation of duty to them. As separate, independent States in Convention, we made the Constitution of the United States with them; and as separate, independent States, each State acting for itself, we adopted it.

South Carolina, acting in her sovereign capacity now thinks proper to secede from the Union. She did not part with her sovereignty in adopting the Constitution. The last thing a State can be presumed to have surrendered is her sovereignty. Her sovereignty is her life. Nothing but a clear, express grant, can alienate it. Inference should be dumb. Yet it is not at all surprising that those who have construed away all the limitations of the Constitution, should also by construction claim the annihilation of the sovereignty of the States. Having abolished all barriers to their omnipotence by their faithless constructions in the operations of the General Government, it is most natural that they should endeavor to do the same toward us in the States. The truth is, they having violated the express provisions of the Constitution, it is at an end as a compact. It is morally obligatory only on those who choose to accept its perverted terms.

South Carolina, deeming the compact not only violated in particular features, but virtually abolished by her Northern confederates, withdraws herself as a party from its obligations. The right to do so is denied by her Northern confederates. They desire to establish a despotism, not only omnipotent in Congress, but omnipotent over the States; and as if to manifest the imperious necessity of our secession, they threaten us with the sword, to coerce submission to their rule.

Citizens of the Southern States of the United States, circumstances beyond our control have placed us in the van of the great controversy between the Northern and Southern States.

We would have preferred that other States should have assumed the position we now occupy. Independent ourselves, we disclaim any design or desire to lead the councils of the other Southern States. Providence has cast our lot together, by extending over us an identity of pursuits, interests, and institutions. South Carolina desires no destiny separated from yours. To be one of a great confederacy, stretching its arms over a territory larger than any Power in Europe possesses -- with population four times greater than that of the whole United States when they achieved their independence of the British Empire -- with productions which make our existence more important to the world than that of any other people inhabiting it -- with common institutions to defend, and common dangers to encounter -- we ask your sympathy and confederation. While constituting a portion of the United States, it has been your statesmanship which has guided it in its mighty strides to power and expansion. In the field, as in the Cabinet, you have led the way to its renown and grandeur. You have loved the Union, in whose service your great statesmen have labored, and your great soldiers have fought and conquered -- not for the material benefits it conferred, but with the faith of a generous and devoted chivalry. You have long lingered and hoped over the shattered remains of a broken Constitution. Compromise after compromise, formed by your concessions, has been trampled under foot by your Northern confederates. All fraternity of feeling between the North and the South is lost, or has been converted into hate; and we of the South are at last driven together by the stern destiny which controls the existence of nations. Your bitter experience of the faithlessness and rapacity of your Northern confederates may have been necessary to evolve those great principles of free government, upon which the liberties of the world depend, and to prepare you for the grand mission of vindicating and re-establishing them.

We rejoice that other nations should be satisfied with their institutions. Self-complacency is a great element of happiness, with nations as with individuals. We are satisfied with ours. If they prefer a system of industry in which capital and labor are in perpetual conflict -- and chronic starvation keeps down the natural increase of population -- and a man is worked out in eight years -- and the law ordains that children shall be worked only ten hours a day -- and the sabre and bayonet are the instruments of order -- be it so. It is their affair, not ours. We prefer, however, our system of industry, by which labor and capital are identified in interest, and capital, therefore, protects labor; by which our population doubles every twenty years; by which starvation is unknown, and abundance crowns the land; by which order is preserved by unpaid police, and the most fertile regions of the world where the Caucasian cannot labor are brought into usefulness by the labor of our own people, and the whole world is blessed by our own productions. All we demand of other peoples is to be let alone to work out our own high destinies. United together, and we must be the most independent, as we are the most important among the nations of the world. United together, and we require no other instrument to conquer peace than our beneficent productions. United together, and we must be a great, free and prosperous people, whose renown must spread throughout the civilized world, and pass down, we trust, to the remotest ages. We ask you to join us in forming a confederacy of Southern States."[58]

The reason I include these powerful words, which have been edited by me to highlight the emphasis on South Carolina's correlation of undue influence on the Federal government to Great Britain's treatment of the original colonies, is that when an all-powerful Federal Agency-government can coerce free enterprise to comply with regulations and to submit fees and pay fines to unwillingly supply funding to those same oppressive Agencies, there is an equal and opposite government that will rise against that government. That rising government will not be harmonious. That rising government will be elected and will represent the citizens of the State and local communities.

The States legislatures are close to the local people and are more facilitated by the will of Main Street, as opposed to Wall Street. Serving in the State capitol is not even close to the culture of Washington. There are far fewer cameras and no compunction of custom in the States to allow dynasties to crystallize from apathy. Virtue is gained by many acts and lost by only one, on the State level. Not so in Washington. Apparently, one simply has to refuse to resign in order to keep the office of a U.S. Congressman or a Senator.

The States are alone in their plight in the year 2012. Each State must declare on its own to declare sovereignty. A sovereign state (or simply state) is classically defined as a state with a defined territory on which it

---

[58] Library of Congress *Edward McPherson's Political History of the United States of America During the Great Rebellion*

exercises internal and external sovereignty, a permanent population, a government, and the capacity to enter into relations with other sovereign states.[59]   It is also normally understood to be a state which is neither dependent on nor subject to any other power or state.

As of the writing of this book, there are 40 States who have either passed or debated Sovereignty Acts. It took two years for the State of North Carolina to do so. It was passed on February 11, 2011 and the resolution reads as follows:

"H34-v-1

A HOUSE RESOLUTION SUPPORTING THE STATE OF NORTH CAROLINA'S RIGHT TO CLAIM SOVEREIGNTY OVER CERTAIN POWERS UNDER THE TENTH AMENDMENT TO THE CONSTITUTION OF THE UNITED STATES.

Whereas, the Tenth Amendment to the Constitution of the United States reads as follows: "The powers not delegated to the United States by the constitution, nor prohibited by it to the states, are reserved to the states, respectively, or to the people;" and
Whereas, the Tenth Amendment defines the total scope of federal power as being that specifically granted by the Constitution of the United States and no more; and
Whereas, the scope of power defined by the Tenth Amendment means that the federal government was created by the states specifically to be an agent of the states; and

---

[59] Shaw, Malcolm Nathan (2003). *International law*. Cambridge University Press. p. 178. "Article 1 of the Montevideo Convention on Rights and Duties of States, 1933 lays down the most widely accepted formulation of the criteria of statehood in international law. It note that the state as an international person should possess the following qualifications: '(a) a permanent population; (b) a defined territory; (c) government; and (d) capacity to enter into relations with other states'" Jasentuliyana, Nandasiri, ed. (1995). *Perspectives on international law*. Kluwer Law International. p. 20. "So far as States are concerned, the traditional definitions provided for in the Montevideo Convention remain generally accepted."

Whereas, today, in 2011, the states are demonstrably treated as agents of the federal government; and

Whereas, many federal mandates are directly in violation of the Tenth Amendment to the Constitution of the United States; and

Whereas, Section 4 of Article IV of the Constitution of the United States says, "The United States shall guarantee to every state in this union a republican form of government," and the Ninth Amendment states that "The enumeration in the constitution of certain rights, shall not be construed to deny or disparage others retained by the people;" and

Whereas, the United States Supreme Court ruled in New York v. United States, 112 S. Ct. 2408 (1992), that Congress may not simply commandeer the legislative and regulatory processes of the states; and

Whereas, a number of proposals from previous administrations and some now pending from the present administration and from Congress may further violate the Constitution of the United States; Now, therefore,

Be it resolved by the House of Representatives:

SECTION 1. The North Carolina House of Representatives supports the State's right to claim sovereignty under the Tenth Amendment to the Constitution of the United States over all powers not otherwise enumerated and granted to the federal government or reserved to the people by the Constitution of the United States.

SECTION 2. The North Carolina House of Representatives urges the federal government, as the agent of the State, to cease and desist, effective immediately, mandates that are beyond the scope of any constitutionally delegated powers.

SECTION 3. The North Carolina House of Representatives further urges that compulsory federal legislation which directs states to comply under threat of civil or criminal penalties or sanctions or requires states to pass legislation or lose federal funding be prohibited or repealed."

Utah had a rather mundane 2012 State legislative session, with the exception of the State Sovereignty Bill. Most people do not know that since it's admission into the union, the Federal government has owned more than 70% of its State land. President Clinton declared a million more acres, which happened to have prime low-sulfur coal deposits, off limits to State enterprise. Left with nothing much more that salt and red rocks, the legislators are finally acting to reclaim their State from the Federal agency-government. Here is what was published in the Salt Lake Tribune:

> "...In the $13 billion budget, which saw about $440 million in new spending, lawmakers were good to education, law enforcement, state employees and social services.
> But it was the state sovereignty-palooza, including Utah's Sagebrush Rebellion 2.0, that garnered the most attention, as lawmakers sought to stake a claim to 30 million acres of federal land in the state with an eye toward instigating a court fight.
> Conservative Republicans also waged a war over educational curriculum standards Utah and other states joined, which they viewed as a federal power grab. And the Legislature joined a health care compact with four other states, asking the federal government to cede health care programs to the state.
> "A message has been sent. That's part of why we're doing it. But we sent a message last year and we send a message most every year," said Senate President Michael Waddoups, R-Taylorsville. "I think the weight of the message is starting to build, though."
> Waddoups said he hears similar frustration from his colleagues in places like Idaho, Arizona, Ohio and other states.
> "We're joining the cacophony of sounds that is coming from the legislatures around this country saying: 'Washington, enough is enough,' " he said.
> But making a statement is very different from making a change, points out Thad Hall, a political science professor at the University of Utah.
> The bills the legislators passed — whether demanding the federal government surrender lands in the state, or give up

running health care — all require Congress to act. Failing that, they don't accomplish much."[60]

It was a weak bluff, but the fact that legislators stood up to the Federal agency-government and told them, "This is our land," sounds a little like Jake Sully telling the Navi people to declare their sovereignty as a united body against the imperial mercenaries sent by corporate Earth to exploit the rare and powerful element *unobtainium*.[61]

Utah seeks to earn a place before the Supreme Court in reclaiming their lands. Other States hope to do the same thing on the subjects of health care, road maintenance, education, and other State functions that have been summarily seized by the agency-government. The States are hoping for a nice, clean legal struggle. It will make for a nice reelection campaign item.

I am getting the feeling, as I hear the speeches and see the spirit of secession behind the letters of the words in these various declarative acts, that there will be a standoff between the State militias—now under the complete control of the Secretary of Defense—and the Federal armies. The uniforms look identical, but the patches on the shoulders will be quite different. The mystery is whether the hearts beating next to those gunstocks will break for liberty moments before pulling that first trigger.

There was a quote that was thrown around in the 1960's when people were beginning to protest the Viet Nam War, which really wasn't a war according to Ron Paul. The quote was this: "What if they threw a war and nobody came?"

---

[60] *2012 Utah Legislature adjourns; focus on sovereignty 2012 session » Theme of Utah legislators' work was to say to Washington: "Enough is enough."*
The Salt Lake Tribune By Robert Gehrke First Published Mar 08 2012 11:23 pm • Last Updated Mar 09 2012 05:15 pm

[61] Jake Sully speech before the Tree of Souls to the Navi people on the planet Pandora. *Avatar* 2010 written, produced, and directed by James Cameron.

It sounds good. It sounds so good that I wanted to know the true source of the quote. It is always good to consider great thoughts in context. Here is the entire poem by Bertolt Brecht, written in the 1930's.

"What if they gave a war and nobody came?
Why, then, the war would come to you!
He who stays home when the fight begins
And lets another fight for his cause
Should take care:
He who does not take part
In the battle will share in the defeat.
Even avoiding battle will not avoid battle.
Since not to fight for your own cause
Really means
Fighting on behalf of your enemy's cause."

This is really a compressed statement against apathy. To vegetate with your smart phone in your lap will be the same as throwing your fist into the air and screaming the oppressor's dehumanizing chant. To smile in a dope-induced stupor and claim you have no idea who is vice-president, or to vote for the politician who promises to make rich corporate folks pay your rent payments is the same as dive-bombing streets full of peaceful protestors.

The States are sovereign entities that have a Federal arrangement that simply allows them to drive across the next border. It allows someone in Indianapolis to sell a car on E-bay to someone in Arkansas. It allows your driver's license to be valid from state to state. It does not mean that the Environmental Protection Agency can pass a regulation with the force of law that shuts down the construction of a new coal-fired power plant that the governor has funded and approved.

There are two things that unite states to work together. The first is commerce. The second is an assault by the Federal agency-government upon state-legal activities conducted on private properties owned by State residents. One State cannot stand against the Secretaries of the President. History has shown us that it will take more than 13 States to do so. As of the writing of this book it is evident that at least 40 States have declared their sovereignty. Now, what will it take to mount a defense that can hold the line against the agency-government led by the Executive Branch?

Since I am writing this book, I choose not to consider violence of any kind. Even passive protests will put people in the way of the agency-government troops. You will suffer chemical spray, severe beatings with clubs, or have your teeth broken by having your head stomped by steel toed boots. You will have your picture taken. Even if no one touches you in any way, your picture and identity will be added to an international database of potentially violent enemies of the agency-government. You may never be able to fly as a passenger on an airline again. You may never be able to qualify for any government aid of any kind. Thousands of Tea Party members are being audited or closely reviewed by the IRS and other government agencies this year alone. I would therefore suggest that you do not join any march against any agency. It does not work in this country any more.

There is no possible way that any type of election can change anything. Representatives of the Republic have no power to even get any agency to answer a single question. In fact, it is illegal for a Congressman or a Senator to even speak to an agency about a constituent's application to do business with the government through that agency.[62] There is only one thing that the States are empowered to do by the Constitution. It is the single, most powerful tool at their disposal. There is no defense against it. It is 100% effective, and it has been used only 17 times since the first document was narrowly ratified on June 21, 1788.

The procedure is called a Constitutional Convention. This process is so powerful and so unpredictable, as designed by the Constitution itself, that if is not handled carefully it could result in the complete destruction of America. Still, it is the only weapon that will save the Republic. The Agency-government has become so powerful that it can circumvent Congress and attack the States directly using the full power of the Federal Executive Branch. No State can withstand such a massive display of

---

[62] The Procurement Integrity Act (41 U.S.C. §423, implemented at FAR 3.104)

power. They command troops, judges, soldiers, and scores of financial agents who can seize wealth within seconds and bring an entire State to a standstill in a matter of hours.

There are loud and generally annoying calls for a Constitutional Convention to be held on July 4th, 2012 in Philadelphia. Although I applaud the amateur left jab at statesmanship, this display of gosh opportunism gives most people a rash.

The Governors of each State with a fully ratified Sovereignty Act on their books can appoint an Athenian delegation made of an equal number of delegates from each state. There can be one or two or twenty, but the larger the number, the greater the temptation of a cacophonous debate collapsing into a brawl.

There must be a clear and concise set of Amendments to the Constitution drafted. The precision and accuracy of the language can be completed and approved ahead of the Convention. There is a strong suggestion to repeal several Amendments that have served their purpose and are no longer necessary. The following is a list of Amendments that must be repealed in order for the Republic to survive and prosper.

Repeal the Following Amendments of the Constitution

- The 16th Amendment: **Passed by Congress: 2 July 1909 Ratified: 3 February 1913**

  The Congress shall have power to lay and collect taxes on incomes, from whatever source derived, without apportionment among the several States, and without regard to any census or enumeration.

- The 17th Amendment: **Passed by Congress: 13 May 1912 Ratified: 8 April 1913**

The Senate of the United States shall be composed of two Senators from each State, elected by the people thereof, for six years; and each Senator shall have one vote. The electors in each State shall have the qualifications requisite for electors of the most numerous branch of the State legislatures.

When vacancies happen in the representation of any State in the Senate, the executive authority of such State shall issue writs of election to fill such vacancies: Provided, that the legislature of any State may empower the executive thereof to make temporary appointments until the people fill the vacancies by election as the legislature may direct.

This amendment shall not be so construed as to affect the election or term of any Senator chosen before it becomes valid as part of the Constitution.

- The 27th Amendment: **Passed by Congress: 25 September 1789 Ratified: 7 May 1992**

No law, varying the compensation for the services of the Senators and Representatives, shall take effect, until an election of representatives shall have intervened.

That's pretty simple, isn't it? Three Amendments need to be repealed. That's all.

Now, there is still some work to do. I have served in management of several corporations and financial ventures. You may have as well. There is one thing that we all know. No company can remain in business if it continues to spend more than it earns. Even the Federal government is bound by this simple rule of economics.

As of the writing of this book, Europe is about $100 trillion dollars in debt, and the entire economy totals to about $70 trillion. Even a child can see there is no possible way the math can work out. Europe is doomed to fail as a union of country-states. The jury does not need to come in on this one. Greece, Spain, Italy, have collapsed and France, Belgium, and perhaps others will fall as well. The people have simply voted for themselves so much of the State's revenue that there is not enough to even keep the banks solvent.

There is still time to fix America, but not much. We have about 24 months before complete collapse of the dollar. The entire business finance world has been corrupted and must be repaired. Remember, the focus is the Agency-government coup d' tat that took your liberties away. This is what needs to be fixed, and there is only one other way besides the one I am proposing with this book. That other way, is the subject of someone else's book. Not this one. We can do this the Constitutional way. Here we go.

Amendments to be Passed and Ratified at the Constitutional Convention

It's true. The following Amendments can be drafted, approved on the State level, passed in the Convention, and ratified by a two-thirds majority all in one day. The entire process can be completed without any problems whatsoever.

- **The 28th Amendment:** No agency, department, or bureau shall exist under the Federal government nor will the regulations created by them have any force of law in any State where that regulation is not ratified by the State legislature. Congress shall represent the citizens of their sovereign States and shall govern the agencies, departments, administrations, and bureaus. Further, the Legislative Branch shall have sole purview and accountability over the agencies, departments, administrations, and bureaus.

- **The 29th Amendment:** The President shall have a cabinet of advisors serving at his will, none of whom can officiate in any capacity in any agency, department, administration, or bureau. These individuals shall be barred from private or public service with any agency, department, administration, or bureau conducting business for or with the Federal government for a period of no less than 5 years. During their service, they shall further be barred from holding any ownership, options, or promise of ownership in any publicly-traded company, or in any company that becomes publicly traded for a period of 5 years after their service in the executive cabinet.

- **The 30th Amendment:** The Congress shall have power to lay and collect taxes on any transaction of commerce wherein currency is the form of trade. The rate shall be uniform for all commerce conducted in the several States without exemption. The tax shall be collected at the point of sale and rendered unto the United States Treasury no more than 30 days from the day of the transaction. Congress shall not have the power to lay and collect taxes from income or profits.

- **The 31st Amendment:** The Senate of the United States shall be composed of two Senators from each State, elected by the people thereof, for six years; and each Senator shall have one vote. No Senator shall serve more than three terms, either consecutively or cumulatively. The electors in each State shall have the qualifications requisite for electors of the most numerous branch of the State legislatures.

When vacancies happen in the representation of any State in the Senate, the executive authority of such State shall issue writs of election to fill such vacancies: Provided, that the legislature of any State may empower the executive thereof to make temporary appointments until the people fill the vacancies by election as the legislature may direct.

This amendment shall not be so construed as to affect the election or term of any Senator chosen before it becomes valid as part of the Constitution.

- **The 32nd Amendment:** The Congress of the United States shall be composed by proportion to represent each State, elected by the people thereof, for four years; and each Congressman shall have one vote. No Congressman shall serve for more than three terms, either consecutively or cumulatively. The electors in each State shall have the qualifications requisite for electors of the most numerous branch of the State legislatures.

When vacancies occur in the representation of any State in the Congress, the executive authority of such State shall issue writs of election to fill such vacancies: Provided, that the legislature of any State may empower the executive thereof to make temporary appointments until the people fill the vacancies by election as the legislature may direct.

This amendment shall not be so construed as to affect the election or term of any Congressman chosen before it becomes valid as part of the Constitution.

- **The 33rd Amendment:** The President shall have the authority to review any bill sent for his signature, and to veto any portion of that bill. He shall report the line items vetoed to the American people, unless the reporting of such items shall harm the security of the United States.

- **The 34th Amendment:** The States shall have the command of their own militias and their national guards. No State shall be compelled to conscribe its militia or its national guards, but shall be free to choose service by its own consensus and sovereignty.

This is not an exhaustive list of Amendments. There are numerous Acts in the chapter *Sovereignty* that can address the other powerful issues of our Republic. Some of these issues may be resolved with legislation, but the above listed items must be done by Amendment, as they then cannot be undone by wealth or corruption. Each of these amendments is powerful, but together they will prevent the imbalance of Powers that we see today.

The Executive Branch has become the monarchy that the founding fathers feared most. The unfunded mandates of the Presidents' Ministers have led us to ruin and devastation. The Congressional dynasties that perpetrate oppression upon the States can be ended forever only by passing all of the Amendments listed above. If we leave any of these out of the set, the balance of power is upset, and tyranny will continue.

World Peace

Amelie's hot chocolate is the key to world peace. If you are ever in Charlotte, North Carolina you must visit Amelie's French Bakery. Tell them I sent you. It's alright. Anytime will do. They're open 24 hours a day on every day of the year. Order the hot chocolate. You will know exactly what I mean.

In my many interviews for this book I have asked people where they thought peace would be impossible. Without variation, they claimed peace was impossible in the Middle East. They all agreed, however, that if peace could be accomplished in the Middle East that world peace was actually possible and even likely.

During the 2007 presidential election cycle, Ron Paul lit a fuse of liberty that became the Tea Party. The momentum was not enough to overcome the steamship of Republican tradition, but the ripple reached Egypt and burst forth as the Arab Spring in Tehrir Square. Smiling and happy millions poured into the streets and demanded the resignation of Hosni Mubarak. For three decades, he squandered countless billions of dollars on a lavish lifestyle, while his nation suffered in poverty.

Without weapons or a heart for violence, the people flashed like starlings in a new direction in January of 2011. Within 18 days, the despotic president left town with his family, taking $84 billion in national funds with him. There was rejoicing in the people. Naïve citizens yelled, "We have won." Careful turbans plotted with their endorsements to seize power. A year later, at the writing of this book, there are still tents in Tahrir Square. They are the custodians of the revolution. They protest in shifts, occupying the Square like continuous watchmen, applying the energy for a republic. Peaceful and sweet people have been beaten and even killed as casually as one might sweep leaves off the porch by the military, who are acting as police. In America, we have police acting like the military so it should be easy for you to understand.

There are voices that are loud and eloquent and have been heard and popularized. Some are writing history; both political and social. Egypt has never had a woman run for office, although there were supposed to be reserved seats in the parliament for females. The military party controls the majority and has ended that reservation, because no *virgins* worthy of holding the office could be found.

One woman is gaining ground, however, though no one gives her a chance. But the prospect of an unveiled woman becoming president of Egypt in an election battle with a dozen Islamic male candidates is making headlines internationally. It's just that in Egyptian newspapers, former radio personality and television news anchor Bothaina Kamel, the first and only woman to run for Egypt's presidency, is usually referred to only as an "activist" — if she is ever referred to at all.

"Some people have come up to me and asked, 'Is it even legal for a woman to run?'" she says. "I hope to set a trend, to open a door."
For nearly a year now, the 49-year-old brunette has been actively campaigning across Egypt, meeting people face-to-face in small rallies and arguing that Egypt needs a social revolution in addition to a political one.[63]

Peace in the Middle East began with Ron Paul in America. Liberty is a universal treasure. It is not a liberty to kill or oppress. It is a liberty to live and seek happiness. When a soul reaches maturity, it reaches a threshold of charity and consideration. How does a soul reach maturity? Well, that is the subject of another book. Let's just say that some of you have come back to help mankind step back from the cliff and live. We can do this. It is within our reach.

I guess we need to hear a candidate tell us that he wants our support so he or she can go to Washington and *work* for us. Hardly a campaign day goes by that we are promised they will go to Washington to *fight* for us. Fight? No. We don't want you to fight anyone. We want you to work for us. Carry our message to them. When the messages are gathered from across the nation into the sample bowl of the Republic, the statistics will be easy

---

[63] Unveiled female former television broadcaster aims to bring a social revolution to Egypt in run for president National Post: by Peter Goodspeed Mar 30, 2012 – 11:24 PM ET

to measure. The constitutional system is designed to protect the individual from the majority, while allowing the proper majority to ratify a federal condition.

In this chapter, we are particularly focused upon the right of States to govern their own affairs, manage their own utilities, collect and distribute their own taxes, and establish commerce for their people. The division between the States has not been an issue for over 200 years. The division between the States and the Federal government is the issue. We have fought many wars in many lands over the millennia about this subject. This time, we will resolve our differences peacefully. This time the States will inform the agency-government that their services are no longer required. It will be the largest stack of pink slips ever mailed out.

Hundreds of thousands of government workers are about to lose their jobs. I can see you're heartbroken about that. Not to worry though. The process will free up trillions of dollars throughout the banking system, which will make funds available for lending to small businesses who will provide better and more productive jobs for those very same former Federal employees.

The States are united. The States are the muscle and brains of this nation. Over the centuries, the individual voters abdicated their own care and feeding to the Federal government, which in turn created an agency-government to handle the job. That new body is not elected, has no accountability to anyone, including the voters, and it is time to remove them from the property.

The votes at this Constitutional Convention do not have to be tallied in Europe by some private software firm. There are only 37 of them needed. We can do that the old fashioned way. 37 Delegates simply need to raise their hands and say "Aye!"

One Small Step

Some of you remember the day when man first stepped onto the Moon. My eyes were glued to my aunt's black and white TV mounted in a Hi Fi console. It was a time when the nation had a focus on that one small step from the last rung of Eagle's ladder to the surface of another world. President Kennedy was an Irish Catholic redhead with an amazing New England accent that seemed to draw everyone into the whirlwind of his expression. He wasn't like a Roman emperor who sponsored State games to keep the people amused while he put the people's wealth up his nose. He was a leader.

I remember someone telling me the difference between a leader and a manager. A manager does things right, and a leader does the right thing. In those days, America was caught up in a cold war. After World War II, the spoils of technology, exasperated people, and entire countries burned into desolation were up for grabs. The Soviets were trying to become the new British Empire, and the Americans chose themselves to be the neighborhood watch to keep them from doing it. After all, America was the only nation that never saw the sole of a foreign soldier's boot nor heard the growl of guns from an airplane over its streets. American factories ran around the clock without a single interruption from its enemies. Somehow the oceans were like a wormhole that only we had the codes for passing through freely. The war was *over there*. The cold war seemed to press the possibility onto our consciousness like the fear of a great dragon lurking silently in a sleepless vigil as though waiting for an inattentive moment in which to turn the party into cinders.

I remember the drills at school. The horn would blare, and we would roll under our desks and put our hands over our heads. Looking back, it was about as effective as holding a tissue up to stop a charging bull. It would have at least have provided a millisecond of beauty to stand out on the playground and watch the initial blast with wide open eyes. Either way, it would have ended the human presence again on Earth for thousands of years. Truly, the Mutually Assured Destruction strategy was insane. I suppose it was a good thing both super-powers were insane at the same time. I mean, what nation in their right mind would ever actually use a nuclear weapon against a city full of people?

The clarity I gained having served in the Air Force at the tropical paradise of Grand Forks Air Force Base in North Dakota established a curiosity about national defense policy that never ended. In fact, what I am about to tell you may shock you. It isn't meant to. I only want you to realize that the game mastered after World War I by Dawes and Young with their financial windfall of making enormous profits by selling machines and weapons to both sides has been refined to a level beyond the imagination. It changed the world in only a few years. Ancient history proves it works this way every time it is employed. We're going to go there in this chapter; beyond your imagination. Don't worry. You'll be traveling with me.

The MAD battle plan was so carefully played out by all the enemies in the cold war that it became abundantly clear that the first one to strike, wins. In the battle plan, both sides placed short-range nuclear weapons hidden off shore of their enemy's command and control headquarters. 80% of the world's population lives within 20 miles of a coast, and for goodness sake the U.S. capitol was within a couple of flying minutes from the Atlantic Ocean. The next step was to design a massive Electromagnetic Pulse (EMP) weapon. It doesn't reach the ground. This weapon was designed to produce a 50-megaton pulse and would simply be housed in the cargo bay of an ordinary aircraft, flying an ordinary airway route and flown at an altitude of about 40 thousand feet.

Somewhere around the epicenter of all electrical grids in the Northeast, a split-second ballet would take place. You can play some Lisa Gerrard music here, because there won't be any other sound while this happens. When the pieces were all in place, and the threat was that they were always in place, the following sequence was to unfold.

The EMP weapon explodes at about 8 miles above the Earth. Within seconds, the entire electrical grid shuts down, and all radio communications cease. At nearly the speed of light, all satellites go dark. All power grids go dark. This was designed to happen on a night with light winds from the West, clear skies, and a massive moment of inattention; such as New Year's eve, or Easter Sunday, or Christmas. It wasn't so much the symbolism or the fulfillment of some Nostradamus Quatrain. Rather, it was calculated to be a moment when the people, including the leadership, looked somewhere else.

Within seconds, the offshore, short-range missiles would be launched. No one would know they are coming at mach 6, because all the electricity and phones are already dead. They would strike their targets in about 5 minutes or less. They would be precisely targeted to hit the command and control center such as Washington DC, Los Angeles, Florida, North Carolina, etc. The instant the short-range missiles are launched, the long-range ICBM's would launch. It takes about 30 minutes for these to leave their silos, travel into space, and plunge back to their targets below. Each missile holds numerous warheads. Each warhead is programmed to strike the ability of the enemy to strike back. The missiles are 90% accurate, and important targets were to be hit twice, improving the effectiveness to 99%.

The entire attack would be over in less than 30 minutes. The vast majority of the nation would know nothing about it. Unless you have a missile silo in your back yard, or you live within driving distance of a command and control center, you would simply wake up late in the morning. Your alarm won't go off. Your phones won't work. Your car won't start. No stores are open. The only thing you will hear will be that strange Lisa Gerrard music I started a few paragraphs back. Life will suddenly collapse to a much simpler time. Suddenly, 300 million people will be on their own.

There will be no counter-strike. The aggressor will issue an immediate cease-fire order, offering peace. There won't be any invasion. No troops will ever set foot in the other country. The loser will have more important things to think about. In less than an hour they will be a third-world country. When the milk sours in the markets, and people run out of cereal and bread and soup and water, they will begin to move. I saw this happen first hand. I was in the 1969 Earthquake at Selmar, California. Our little Simi Valley in California was isolated from the city. Our water was off. Groceries were seized by the Red Cross, and the national guard sealed off the canyon road. The aftershocks kept us all sleepless for days.

Fortunately, the utilities were restored within a couple of days. What would have happened if the utilities did not come back for two years?

This was the cold war. The public did not know this. We were led to believe that we could somehow knock out those evil missiles and that we would be able to strike back and win a nuclear exchange. It simply was not true. Likewise, it was not true for the Soviets as well. There was a subtle and powerful unknown that kept us safe during those years. The Soviets did not know what President Kennedy would do. Would he attack first?

The Soviets decided to hedge their bets by placing missiles with an ally in Cuba. Our spy planes photographed the whole thing, and President Kennedy didn't pick up the red phone for a private chat. He went to the television and told them that if they did not turn around those cargo ships, we would declare war on them. The fact that you are peacefully reading this book is a testament that they did turn around and go home. Soviet submarines would have to be the forward launch points from then on. For another 25 years, silent tubes of titanium were submerged with ready commanders trained to carry out the short-range attacks on a moment's notice. The EMP blast never announced the runners could leap out of their starting blocks. The race lost interest and ran out of money.

Here we are in the 21st century with no army to fight. Thank God those days are over forever. So, why are we still spending $1.3 trillion annually on national defense? That is one of the greatest questions of the millennium. Why indeed. Rather than soil my shoes by walking down the conspiracy path, I am going to offer an experiment. Since I live by the scientific method, let's form a hypothesis, and experiment to prove or disprove the hypothesis, and form a theory which may later become an axiom for human civilization.

America currently has 50 States and a few territories who want to become States and a few States that no longer want to be. There are about 300 million people with about that many realities as well. There is an average reality that we call mortal life. Humans have a productive lifespan of about 80 years, removing pre-adolescence and the tarnished portion of the golden years from the equation. 50 is the new 30, you know.

Okay, let's state the hypothesis: "A peaceful human race through extreme challenge, unlimited education, and adequate food, water, and facilities."

There are already a few facts that we have gathered from empirical evidence that will help with the design of the experiment. We watched America pull together and focus technology and national will on the race to the Moon. We take it for granted now, but technology has scarcely utilized transistors when the first space launches were accomplished. Did you know that Ranger 4 missed the Moon by 37,000 miles? Space scientists know how to compensate by subtracting the *extra energy* supplied by rotational access to extra-dimensional torsion, but most do not know how to capitalize on that energy. Not yet, anyway. We also know that nearly all the funding for the space program originates with the industrial military complex. Yes it exists. It also spends far more than $1.3 trillion a year on national defense, but there is no easy way to discover exactly how much is spent, or the results of the spending. That, too, is the subject of another book.

We also know a couple of other facts. Nearly every nation spends money on national defense. This is where the experiment is going to get interesting. Remember when Kennedy applied his leadership to place America on the Moon within a decade? Why? I suppose, and this is a scientific supposition, that humans are explorers first and not warriors by nature. I think *lover* is ranked in there somewhere as well.

With that supposition, here is the experiment. What would happen if America applied 75% of its defense budget, which is about $975 billion—officially speaking, of course—a year, to the exploration and colonization of the Moon? This is a radical shift in the application of funding. This is more money than has ever been applied to any effort, other than buying votes or conquering people.

This would require some resources in people; scientists, engineers, and skilled technicians to invent and manufacture everything. The Moon has plenty of water and oxygen, but they're locked up in the soil. The Moon has no protective magnetosphere and very little atmosphere, so accommodations would have to be built under the surface. Okay. You get the picture of how large the challenge would be. It fits the criteria for extreme challenge, to be sure.

We can estimate that there will be some effects very similar to what Kennedy must have predicted when he was sitting in his top-secret committee discussing his Moon-landing idea. He must have thought that it would make the Soviets catch the vision as well. "Hey wait a minute. What if they claim the Moon? What's up there? What do they know that we do not?" The Soviets were rubbing their hands together and fretting over whether to build more missiles or build more rockets to explore space.

One thing is irrefutable. Every expert agrees on this. He, who controls the Moon, shall control the Earth. If America were to turn its budget for breaking things and killing people into one of national exploration and colonization of space, the entire world would change. Why do I say that? Because it will take much more than American brain power and money to make this happen.

It will take Indian, Chinese, Japanese, Iranian, Iraqi, and Israeli engineers and scientists and money to make it happen. If we can conduct this experiment, there will be a global focus on extreme challenge that will require an unlimited amount of educated people. Educated people do not allow their social groups to grow beyond the environment's ability to support them. It is a biological fact that populations that grow too far in their environment will express warlike attributes. Rats, birds, and even bacteria display the same phenomena. Humans are intelligent and have will and desire, which animals do not. We do not need predators to limit our population the way rabbits and coyotes do. We can choose to limit our own growth to match our environment. We can plan for the future of our society, and the further into the future we plan, the more successful we will be as a race upon this or any other planet.

If we are focused as a planet on exploration and colonization of space, we are not killing each other. Besides that, it is much more fun to explore and live to tell about it. The discoveries and proliferation of technology necessary to propel and sustain humans into space will benefit the environment as well. We may be able to stop burning petroleum for transportation. We may be able to produce inexpensive clean drinking water from the sea, forming the first complete reusable water supply. We may be able to cheaply convert solar energy into electricity which will allow our society to break away from the wired grid that forces us to live in concentrated areas. My company already utilizes a 1.4 square meter solar panel that outperforms anything the solar industry has ever seen. I can't give you any more details here without a signed nondisclosure statement by you. My associates haven't even gotten started yet.

As long as we are challenged as a race, we will not seek the destruction of one another. We are immensely powerful and intelligent beings. From the earliest days this biological transducer has walked this planet and allowed us to interpret the universe through its senses, we have looked up into the stars. As though longing to remember the way home, we have written songs and danced beneath them. We have pointed and wondered and even imagined what it would be like. Perhaps it is because we don't remember. Perhaps the spirit inside the body has existed beyond universes and has seen stars born, grow old, and die. Perhaps we are connected to the 96% of the universe we cannot perceive from this dimension. If we already explored the universe and chose Earth for the home of our children's children, why would we treat her so?

I am proposing to save a nation with this book. I ask you to reach down inside the universe folded up in each of you and find the knowledge that peace and liberty can and must exist for mankind. I ask you to convene and to remove the agency-government that sees the human race as sheep to be shorn. You are not sheep. You are a leaping, flying being without fear and with a capacity for love that is godlike. Save America. Save the human race. We have the will and a window of opportunity. Don't listen to the agency-government that only demands your *fair share* to support their lifestyles.

We do not have to step off the cliff into the valley of Armageddon like human races before us on this world. We are empowered with the conditional prediction of that future for the human race through a profit-driven war machine that sends children to kill one another. We can leap back from the edge. We do not have to follow that path. We can choose a new future. We can choose to release the agency-government that is destroying us, and return the power of government to the States where it belongs.

Home Repair Kit

In my travels, people ask me, "What can I do? How can I help?"

This book is designed to awaken you. You are ready to get off the Federal sideshow that has masqueraded as America for more than 80 years. You are ready to hear the inspired voices of the founding fathers. You are ready for liberty. Be prepared for a mess. Oh, I don't mean the mess of trying to return to the true path of unalienable rights and the pursuit of happiness. I mean the mess of cleaning out the dark back rooms of the agency-government. The things we will find when we shake out the sheets and shovel all the crap that has piled up in the closets into a pile to be burned for safety will be sure to turn your stomach.

But, like lancing any festering sore, it must be done to start the healing process. We need new soup lines for the hundreds of thousands of agency-government employees who have to learn how to work for a living. They have atrophied and wasted away to a society that cannot stand up on their own, nor can they speak out for themselves. Government has always done that for them. They will need our help and our charity. This time, the charity will be voluntary and not forced at the point of a gun.

The stimulus to the economy of the world will be phenomenal. Trillions of dollars in value will be released to the market to begin moving again. With tens of thousands of regulations out of the way, such as tax codes and the nation-wide blockade on small businesses, the liberty of America will swell forward like the collapse of a Nordic ice dam. The pent up flow of commerce and progress and innovation will come out of the mountains as the word of God, flowing from the bowls of Earth.

Here are few things you need to do.

Slowly, very carefully, get your cash out of the bank. It is not safe there, because the patient will go through withdrawal convulsions. Trillions of dollars of your savings and checking account money is being high-frequency traded by your bank, while you are not watching. It is exceedingly margined, and when the currency collapse occurs, you will lose all your money, just like the folks at MF Global did when John Corzine and his cronies absconded with their depositors' funds. You don't want to be financially anywhere close when the wailing demons of the agency-government come spewing out of the throat of America as it gasps for new life. You may want to change some of the cash into silver coin. Stay away from gold; especially certificates. They're worthless unless you have the actual metal in your hands. Gold is too valuable and private ownership of it will most likely be outlawed again, once the fact that Fort Knox has nothing in it but IOU's is revealed to the world.

Buy some simple food storage. I suggest high-density dehydrated foods that you can put in the car or load into a backpack. You might want to store some water as well. I suggest the two-liter bottles. They're tough and won't breathe any flavors into them like a milk jug. Don't buy 50-gallon drums of food and don't store water in 5-gallon buckets. You won't be able to move if you have to. If fuel or food stops trading for any reason, there will be a hiccup in food supplies. Having some on hand means you don't have to rely on someone else, least of all FEMA, for your care and feeding.

Get out of debt immediately, if not sooner. Cash in your 401K and take the 10% tax hit if you have to, but pay off everything you can and sell anything you owe money on except your house. Yes, sell your car. Buy a used one. You can't afford a new one if you can't pay cash. I'm sorry, but it will be this way for about two years while things get put back together again. Debt will be slavery. Get free. That includes your student loans. Pay them off in one check. I don't care how cheap the interest rate, you must get out of debt. Live more simply if you have to. Your 401K will splatter like a daisy smacked with a nine-iron if you let the financial firms hold onto it.

Contact your Congressman today by email, website form, or by calling. Tell them you support the declaration of your State's sovereignty from the agency-government. They'll know exactly what you mean. Tell them you are watching them and will vote for a constitutional convention to repeal certain amendments and pass a few more to help define what the founding fathers were talking about. Tell them you want the governor to recall all State militia from foreign wars.

Turn off the news channels. They are propaganda machines designed to herd you like sheep into a certain political corral. Use online news or try communicating with others through mail, email, or blogs to keep yourself free from the company message. If you cannot interact with it, like a phone-in radio program or a town hall meeting—assuming one will actually let your unscreened opinion attend—turn it off. This will dry up the flow of cash to their organizations.

Vote. If you are not registered to vote, get registered. Use your voice to vote and convince others to vote. Do not be swayed by the propagandists that resistance is futile. Envision a future where you are free to start and own a successful business or to have a good-paying job without some agency telling you that you cannot. Our form of government works better than anything ever tried on this planet, but it won't function if you don't stay informed and use your power to vote.

Never give up. We have one last chance to save this republic. If we let apathy win this next election, then we will have lost our republic. Send the Congressional dynasties home for good. Sweep out their offices, shred their house of cards, and let's begin again on liberty's pathway to prevent the agency-government from ever taking root again. We can do this on our own. We do not need government's help.

I applaud you for reading this book. I wrote it for you. I have felt like you needed this for a long time. You had nearly given up hope. It's alright now. Help is on the way.

Peace and joy, my friends,

Brooks Agnew

15786488R00100

Made in the USA
Lexington, KY
16 June 2012